MIKE KIRBY

My Father and Other Animals

Growing up on a Yorkshire Farm

First edition

ISBN: 978-1-3999-7370-0

This book was professionally typeset on Reedsy.
Find out more at reedsy.com

1

A MAN OF FEW WORDS

My father would regularly remind us that our two ears and one mouth should be used in proportion to their number and that it was better to be thought a fool than to open our mouths and prove it. He would rarely use one word where none would do.

He almost never talked about himself, his childhood, his birth family or his early years of work. We suspected that there were painful episodes in his past which he didn't want to revisit. The early loss of his mother must have hit him hard, but she was rarely mentioned. He didn't get on with his dad at all. We would overhear rows between father and son and between Dad and his brother. Dad's family was not close and as we grew up, Dad was increasingly estranged from them and for the last thirty years of his life had no contact. Our two cousins were strangers to us.

To attempt to piece him together, to understand him and what drove him, is like trying to do a jigsaw puzzle with some of the corners and the edges missing. Now he has gone, that helpful picture on the lid of the box is fading.

Dad's focus was always on his farm and the future. He would be deep in thought while he worked: planning, scheming, making mental lists of jobs that needed doing, and coming up with ways to do things better and get the money together to realise his dreams. This thoughtfulness could make him hard to be around. I long to have a proper conversation now. When he was alive, it was just too hard and, sadly, we both gave up trying.

His default expression was half scowl, half inquisitive. The scowl could be taken as a sign of his disapproval, and feeling disapproved of, most of the time, was a hard place to be for his sons and those he worked with. His actual approval was rarely forthcoming.

He joked that his vision was for what he called 'a dog and a stick farm': the dog was to do all the running around and the stick was for him to lean on and watch. But this was a view of the future not suited to his energy and drive. Anyone who took the time to observe him for a while would see constant motion. He walked deliberately and with purpose. He would never amble. He worked towards his ambition every day, action by action, with a single-minded determination, starting early and finishing late.

In his minds eye, he pictured his farm, the buildings, and how it would all work, long before he was able to start making it real. He saw a farm that was a collection of all he had learned, and stored away for future use, about how animals should be bred and housed and fed. He was a magpie collector of useful details; using all he'd learned, he set about building his vision on a grassy slope, leading down to a river, next to where the house, he imagined, would be. He built it one brick at a time, slow and deliberate, but with absolute certainty that he would get there in the end.

In his mind's eye he saw his barns and his fields full of strong cattle, feeding contentedly, and he saw his family, safe, secure, growing, thriving and working together towards the vision that burned so clearly in his mind, but that he was never able to put into words. I suppose he was too busy making it happen to have time to talk about it. His vision was precious and so personal that he just didn't have the words.

The saying goes that farming never stops. Animals are there to be looked after every day, having no respect for holidays, illness, good or bad weather. There could be no more perfect calling for my Father, and no better metaphor for how he lived. The rhythms within the days, weeks, months and seasons of a farming year provided a comforting predictability. The farming life was all he knew and all he wanted to know.

He was blessed with a huge measure of discontent. This was his driving force. Perhaps every now and then he allowed himself to be pleased. If he did, it didn't show. If he ever glimpsed contentment, it would perhaps have been on a warm, still, summer evening, walking his fields with his cattle all around him. Only then might he have allowed himself a smidgen of

3

satisfaction. But I doubt it.

Every morning, looking in the bathroom mirror, my father looks back at me with that familiar part scowl. I might catch my brothers in a sideways glance, a similar furrowed brow, just like he would look at people, side on, as if by facing up to the world, he would reveal more of himself than he wanted. The apples have not rolled far from the tree and all of us are our father's sons.

It was probably when my children came along that the lifelong process of becoming my father's son became fully apparent. I would hear myself and my brothers using words he might have used, applying judgments he would have applied, phrases only he could come out with. It makes me cringe at times when these things come from my mouth, and my children must wonder what on earth I am talking about.

We all retreat into our work with a self-absorption he would recognise and, like him, we always have at least three jobs on the go at once and are resentful of interruptions. We plan and scheme, striving to plot the future, just as he did, most of the time forgetting that the present moment is all we have properly in our control.

All four of his sons are blessed with his drive, his ambition and his love for the work. This is his legacy. When I slip up, I remind myself of the good example set for all of us by this irresistible man. I think how he would chide us all if we wanted an extra ten minutes in bed, or if, having been on our feet all day, we wanted a bit of a sit before heading out again. If I can leave my children a similar legacy, I will have succeeded.

The pieces of the puzzle, some connected to other pieces, some not, come together to form a picture. But sometimes the pieces get isolated, separate, spread across the table, missing connections, leaving us all to guess at what is in the gaps.

This book is a series of snapshots of my father's farming life, from my earliest memories to the realisation of his vision. It is about what shaped my brothers and me, but most of all it is about the sometimes remote, always complex, mischievous, impatient, inaccessible, energetic and relentless man that was our father, about his supernatural powers around his animals, and about his ability to adapt and learn and make mistakes and overcome them.

2

THE KIRBY'S

This is my family:

Dad, Brian, never Daddy (he hated that and we only ever used it to annoy him). Always called Bri by Mum, Alison, who in turn was always called Lal by Dad.

Mum was the daughter and the granddaughter of farmers and all her uncles were farmers too. She studied dairying at university and her first job involved farming. She met my dad in the upstairs room of a pub, where she was giving a talk to a group of farmers about how to improve the quality of the milk they produced. She was deeply practical, patient and optimistic, a constant, stable presence for my father and the family that was to come.

I am the eldest of four boys, christened, but only ever referred to as Michael when I was in trouble. Called Mick by the family, or Our Micky, I was known to everyone else, for most of my life, as Mike. Being the eldest meant that I got to do pretty much everything first: the first one to have a girlfriend home, to crash Dad's car, to visit a pub and the first to roll home drunk from a night out with the lads and leave the back door wide open all night.

I always seemed to get into more trouble than my younger brothers. By the time they were old enough to be stumbling out of pubs on a Friday night, Mum and Dad were pretty much used to it and bollockings never seemed quite as severe for them as they had been for me.

My three younger brothers, in order, are John, Mark and Andrew. Dad would often run through all four names before settling on the son he was actually talking to. For no good reason I ever knew, for years I was called Paddy by Dad, and Dad only. He also called me Flonny. Again, I have no idea why.

John, eighteen months younger than me, would be addressed as Nhoj, a neat reversal of his name. Like both our parents, John was practical in ways I never was. He could fix anything. He studied engineering at college, learning how to make and mend. He inherited our father's economy with words.

Then a small age gap to Mark who has always been and still is known as Sam. The day he was born, we were read a story at school about Little Black Sambo (it would never happen now). Getting home from school to find we had a new baby brother, who had a shock of dark curly hair, meant he was called Sambo or Sam for the rest of his life. Sam's infectious laughter could light up a room.

Andrew was usually Ank, after his initials. Growing up the youngest in a family of four brothers meant he had to try extra hard. This made him even more determined to succeed than the rest of us. He hasn't let severe dyslexia hold him back.

Raised on a farm, we were allowed to roam and, as long as we were back in time for our tea, nobody minded. We developed a love of being outdoors and a cast iron work ethic. We thrived on three big meals a day and all the snacks in between that we could manage.

Mum and Dad were farmers, Mum had farming in her blood. And Dad, who had started with nothing, through the relentless application of common sense and a unique and instinctive set of skills around his animals, made himself the farmer he had wanted to be all his life.

3

TOP OF THE TOWN FARM

Top of the Town Farm was located, as the name suggests, at the top of a hill, along a lane, looking over the village of Thurlstone near Barnsley in South Yorkshire. This was Mum and Dad's first farm, the first place they lived together after they were married, and where John and I were born.

The farm consisted of a foursquare farmhouse, its sandstone building blocks blackened by chimney soot. The house was old and draughty and bitterly cold in the winter, cool in the summer heat. In winter, frost would collect in crazy patterns on the inside of the windows. Thick curtains were hung to stop the cold, and going from a cosy warm bed to fully dressed, required speed. Bedtime meant hot water bottles, curling up on the warm patch in the middle of the bed, before moving the bottle down the bed to warm chilly toes. Thick woollen blankets, piled high for warmth, were comfortingly heavy. In winter, only in the yellowing light of the steamy farmhouse kitchen could you be guaranteed to be warm, the ancient range providing the only source of heat and a place for cooking and to gather round to warm frozen hands, dry wet hats and gloves and take the chill off your wellies.

The house stood in one corner of a rectangle of buildings, and a large stone barn with huge wooden doors was attached directly to the farmhouse. Around the rough yard there were loose boxes for the animals, plus feed and equipment stores. A gate in the corner opposite the house led up a bumpy lane to the stackyard where most of the winter feed was stored and tractors and trailers were parked. The lane led away to the pot-holed single-track road at the top, with a small orchard on the left. In summer the apple trees, heavy with fruit, lolled on the wall and dripped sour windfalls onto the rough stony lane.

From the top of our lane the sky opened out and you could see the higher Pennine hills. When it rained the hills seemed higher; no longer so far distant, they pressed in on the valleys, clouds clinging to the tops. In summer the sky became huge in the sun, the heather coloured the hills pale purple and they looked further away, altogether more friendly, less threatening.

Thurlstone village spilled up the hill from the crowded valley, through which the River Don flowed. The water was a milky brown colour due to the peat from the hills, mixed with the colour of rust from the old, long played-out iron works further up the valley. It would roar down the valley in winter, flush with heavy rain.

The river vied for space with the main road over the Pennines, and the train line from Sheffield to Manchester. Traffic rumbled a few feet away from the front steps of terraced houses, splashing road grime in the rain and blackening painted doors, the muck building up on the window ledges. Front steps were brushed daily and washed as well. On the railway, cut deep into the steep valley sides, trains rumbled by, close behind the houses.

At one time the river had provided power to woollen mills and foundries, but these were long gone by the sixties. The only remaining industry was a maker of carbon products, whose lorries carried black sludge onto the roads. The bottom of the valley seemed narrow, dark and noisy, made damp by the mucky Don and the clatter of the traffic.

The narrowing lane up through the village led to fields hemmed by drystone walls and then open moor beyond. Most of the year this was not an easy place to farm. Heavy, water-logged land was given over to grazing cattle and sheep who turned their backs to the wind, sheltering under the wall sides and churning up the thick black mud in the gateways.

The hillsides were dotted with farmhouses, the walls of thick sandstone, blackened by the smoke from the factories that used to exist in the valley below and the smoke from the coal fires that burned the ample coal from the pits not far away. Low buildings might be huddled around a small open yard offering shelter but little warmth. A crooked Dutch barn, its corrugated metal sheets rusted red-brown and thinning, would stand by the farmyard, bent and flinching from the wind, held up by

11

the bales of straw stacked underneath.

The rain leached much of the goodness from the land and farming these poor thin, acidic soils offered precarious financial reward for all the long hours, the mud, and horizontal rain. Top of the Town was a small farm, but it was a start, a long-held dream for Dad, who –having left school at fourteen – knew little else but farm work. Mum and Dad had saved every penny, cutting corners wherever they could to get the money together to start their own place.

The villages and small towns of South Yorkshire mainly took shelter in the valleys, out of the wind. But at the top of the hill, the air was fresh and the summer light was bright. The wind blew hard at times, bending the few trees to its prevailing will. Bushes were stunted and thin. We were not isolated up there, just separate.

Beyond our farm, the tarmac lanes petered out to stony dirt tracks with even more isolated farms at the end of them. The land was wet all year round and clumps of rushes grew in the bogs.

On the edges, the open moors pressed in on the green of the grass fields. Here the drystone walls had long since tumbled down, the blackened stones now pock-marked with lichen and moss. Rusted iron gates hung from broken hinges. Wind-battered wooden gates came apart where they stood. The sheep often roamed at will, constrained by hastily erected barbed-wire fences on which strands of wool fluttered in the wind. Cattle grids set into the narrow lanes held the animals high on the hill.

Most people from the village worked away in the local towns. There were still some coal pits in driving distance. The village supported a couple of pubs, a church and a chapel and a general store. There was a primary school, and after that 'big school' was a couple of miles away.

Like many high places, the weather in the foothills of the Pennines could be capricious, with all four seasons in one day not unusual. Winters seemed longer and colder and summers longer and warmer back then. We experienced the weather first hand every day at work and at play; our lives involved a lot of outside and most days that meant a lot of weather.

In winter, snow collected against the walls and stayed for months at a time, slowly becoming icy, its edges flecked with soot from the coal fires in the valley. But regardless of the weather – even if we were snowed in – animals still needed to be fed, including ones that spent their days outdoors. Heavy weather meant that sheep would shelter in the lee of the nearest wall. Being particularly stupid animals, this often meant they were sheltering where the deepest drifts of snow were bound to accumulate. A cold snap or a light sprinkling of snow would have them pawing at the frozen ground with their front feet, nibbling at the ends of any grass that poked through. This would never be enough to sustain them, and hay and straw bales would need to be transported to the fields by tractor.

Getting tractors out of the yard was also a challenge sometimes, and much painstaking snow shifting would be required to allow the tractors to move successfully up and down the lanes to the fields.

Dad would pull his flat cap hard down over his forehead, both for warmth and to make sure it didn't blow away. His heavy weather jacket would be secured round the middle with twine from bales of straw, as he set himself to feeding and watering his stock, tasks that would take all day sometimes. The cold would freeze the water pipes to the animals' drinking troughs.

Later, when we moved to a farm at Scout Dike, we kept beef cattle penned in a barn with a feeding passage down the middle so that most of the stock could be fed by tractor, but at Top of the Town everything was done by hand. Cows would need mucking out and steam would rise from the muck heap on cold days. Fresh, bright days with a hard frost were welcomed, a chance to spread some manure on the hard ground and to get tractors into fields without getting bogged down.

For me and my brother, a snowy day or fresh overnight snow meant that it was time to go sledging. There were many ideal places and we would stay out in the snow quite happily until our hands froze and lips turned blue. Mum would fetch us indoors for as long as it took to thaw out. Wet gloves and hats steamed on the kitchen range and damp coats were slung over chair backs to dry quicker so we could do it all again. Rapidly defrosting fingers caused 'hot aches', cheeks tingled and toes throbbed.

Outside again as quickly as we were allowed, sledging meant cracking heads and bruising backsides and ribs. The steep bank sides were ideal for rolling huge snowballs, which sat where they stopped at the bottom of the slope, too heavy to move, lasting for days after the rest of the snow had melted.

Dad hated the wind the most. It could roar and roil down from the high tops and push over stacks of straw, tearing heavy tarpaulins from end to end. The hay and straw, gathered in the summer and carefully stacked and sheeted, would be at the mercy of the elements. Rain turned precious hay bales black and made them impossibly heavy, good only for bedding at best, or the muck heap at worst.

The wind might damage the part-finished roof on Dad's latest building project or even lift sharp-edged galvanised metal sheets clean off the older sheds and send them cartwheeling across the top yard, the cattle sheltering underneath, now getting wet and cold. It would rattle the house windows and lift the tiles on the roof. Farm debris would be scattered, and the chill of the winter wind felt like it might cut you in half.

Rain would come at you on the slant, stinging eyes and uncovered ears. It would quickly fill the deep ruts made by the tractors in the fields, forming pools in hollows and turning the muck and dust in the farmyard to sludge. At Top of the Town, water ran down the track from the top lane, right on through the bottom yard and out through the gate before turning hard left down the road towards the village and the mucky River Don.

The heavy clay soil was ill suited to hold the water in. Walking the fields, you could hear water constantly on the move beneath your feet. Small rills formed, previously dry springs sprung, and the ground squelched under wellies.

In spite of the weather, and sometimes because of it, being outside was where we chose to be. The seasons, marked by changes in the weather, by the early darkness in autumn and the long dark nights of winter, provided an overlay to the rhythms of the farm. Dad said there was no such thing as bad weather, just the wrong clothes. Mum would wrap us up warm for the chill outside, with proper vests, thick shirts and woolly jumpers. Gloves would be attached to elastic, the band fed through each sleeve. As we grew, shorts and long socks were worn whatever the weather, and going outside involved wrapping ourselves tightly in duffle coats, fastening the toggles and pulling hoods over bobble-hatted heads. Hands would be plunged deep into duffel-coat pockets. Dad's idea of a joke was to put a dead mouse he had found in my pocket. My hand would explore this soft furry object before realising what it was. This still gives me shudders. One of his other tricks was to drop something squidgy and revolting into one of my wellies, perhaps even another dead mouse. He thought it hilarious, I less so.

Our close neighbours at Top of the Town were Fred and Doris Smith and their daughter Rita, who lived in the cottage that backed on to the bottom yard. It was an old weaver's cottage, part of a row, with lots of small windows running across the top floor, letting in light so the home workers could see the warp and the weft. The little houses were squat and solid.

Their dark, cosy front room was often my first port of call in the morning. I never knew what Fred did. I never saw him go to work. I am pretty sure he was retired; maybe he had been a miner. He always wore a big heavy wool suit, black, shiny in places and patched with leather at the elbows, a thick gold watch chain draped from a waistcoat pocket. The suit must have been made for the bigger bloke he had once been. He wore a big flat cap, even indoors. Always. Summer and winter.

He sat in a big rocking chair. If he ever moved from this seat, I never saw it. He had huge black leather boots, hob-nailed and laced to the top, above his ankles and always highly polished. They rested never more than twelve inches from the embers of a glowing coal fire, his feet up on a step just in front of the slatted grate.

Fred smoked a pipe. The room was tinged yellow by the smoke from this and the coal fire, and the nets at the window were stained a grim shade of cream. The air was thick with smoke and the smell of the breakfast fry-up, just cleared away. His chair was angled for least effort when it came to being near the fire. He would lean forward to tap out his pipe on the open grate, making the embers momentarily crackle.

Fred could also reach his mug of tea by simply extending a forearm to where it sat, keeping warm on the range – a strong dark brown brew, three sugars. Every now and then he would hawk up whatever was in his throat and with pinpoint accuracy spit into the fire. I was by turns revolted, fascinated and envious of his precision. A satisfying split-second hiss from the fire was accompanied by Fred settling back into his chair.

17

'Na then young un, what you on with today?' Always the same question.

'Just been doing my jobs, Mr Smith.' Always the same answer.

He would reach into the recesses of the huge jacket pocket and out would come two 'spice'.

'One for now and one for tha pocket,' he always said.

'Thank you, Mr Smith,' I would respectfully reply. Mum had taught us flawless politeness.

Sometimes humbugs, wrapped tight and sticky-warm from his pocket, sometimes bright red and yellow rhubarb and custard from a crumpled paper bag, maybe an acid-sweet lemon drop. The spice was all I went for really.

Fred's wife, Doris, was small, round and busy. She fussed constantly around Fred, made up his fire, cooked his breakfast, cleared the dishes and fetched his tea. I never remember seeing either of the Smiths outside this one small room and the adjoining kitchen. I am sure they must have ventured out sometimes, as their garden was a riotous tangle of sweet peas, honeysuckle and pink flowering clematis, tumbling over the front garden wall.

Rita, also small and round, but never busy, sat and knitted, drank tea and chatted to her dad, and commented to her mum when she bustled by with ever more tea.

'How's your mum? one of them might ask.

'And your little brother?'

'What's your dad busy with?'

From me, a series of 'don't knows' and maybe a 'fine, thank you, Mrs Smith'. I was not the most talkative uninvited house guest. I brought no news from the outside world. I stayed just long enough to justify the spice. On cold days I might warm my hands.

The back kitchen was Doris's domain. No cooker in this kitchen, though. Cooking was done on the range, heated by Fred's glowing embers. A lifted lid revealed a hot plate. A freshly stove-blacked door opened to a small oven. On the hot plate, when the kettle was not on, vegetables might bubble, usually cabbage, boiling to mush. Doris tripped back and forth. She didn't seem to mind that Fred sat, all day, unmoved and untroubled, directly in her path.

On the face of it, Dad seemed to have no time for the Smiths. He didn't hold with smoking, spitting or even sitting for that matter. But I think he kept an eye on them. They seemed to have a stability that matched the solid stone walls that they never seemed to venture beyond. A comfortable predictability. He looked out for them, fixed things that broke and passed a few words as he rushed by.

My stays were never long. I had jobs to do and had to be off. 'Just like thy father,' Fred would say. If ever I had cause to return later in the day, I would find them in the same seats, still kalin – their word for chatting, Fred smoking and spitting, Doris fussing and tutting, Rita knitting. This was the world for them. No radio or music or TV to intrude, just the safe and the known and the hum and the bustle of this front room.

Because Top of the Town was not a big farm, Dad also had a day job for the Ministry of Agriculture as a way to make ends meet in the beginning. In spite of his endless energy and long days, the farm was just too big for one man to manage, even with a little 'help' from two small boys. There was willing and able help at hand from the village in the form of John Lockwood, or Lockud as he was known to everyone.

Lockud liked a beer or three or five and often more. He had turned up at Top of the Town Farm as a young kid, older than me, but still at school, when he could be bothered to get out of bed to go. Like Dad, Lockud stuck it at school only as long as he had to. He was a big lad, thick set and strong. He looked older than he was, which probably made the landlord at his 'local' – or any other pub he might be passing – turn a blind eye. He got a taste for the beer at an early age and earned a few bob from Dad to pay for it.

Lockud didn't have a proper job to go to out of school, or any qualifications. The farm was an escape for him; he was young and had energy and was generally willing to help, for something to do, for a few quid out of Dad's back pocket every now and then. Nothing formal, but he would turn up, sometimes for days on end, work, get paid, go to the pub and that would be it for a few days. He never turned up the worse for drink, but Dad often said you could smell it on him. Dad said he was a useful man to attach to a shovel or a muck fork and a good worker, when the spirit moved him.

Sometimes he would turn up with a mate, an even bigger lad, his size making him awkward, shy and always a step or two behind Lockud. We never used his name, everyone called him Thud, for the noise his footfall might make as he moved slowly around. Thud was a watcher rather than a worker, and Lockud would be mucking out a shed while Thud looked on, content to lean on a wall or sit on a straw bale. Thud might wheel the barrow up the yard to the muck heap if he could be bothered.

At harvest time, Lockud and Thud made themselves useful, their strength and stamina tested by heavy bales of hay that needed lifting onto trailers and then offloaded onto the stacks in the top yard. When they had the money, they would not stop for tea, preferring to make their way home via the pub.

Perhaps Dad saw two lost boys who still had homes to go to, but with nothing much to keep them there. Perhaps not unlike himself at that age. So, he took them on, paid them a bit, tolerated their no-shows and tried to give them purpose, perhaps hoping that his work ethic might rub off a little.

4

ANIMALS

My father had an extraordinary intuition when it came to animals. A sense of them, all his own, which only he seemed to posses. He was evacuated from Sheffield to rural Derbyshire aged ten and during the war he lived with the Twigg family, who had a smallholding in a little village near Ashbourne, set deep in the Derbyshire Dales. This was where he must have first encountered farm life. The scant details he provided meant we had to paint our own picture of the Twigg family, living cheek by jowl with their animals in the Derbyshire countryside, sheep quietly grazing on the village green, limestone walls snaking away from the villages up the steep valley sides, bees buzzing and the sun always shining.

The rural peace of it belied the war raging, sometimes, close by. Squadrons of German bombers flew over every night, trying to wipe Sheffield – with its steel mills and iron foundries – off the map. This was Dad's home town and where his parents lived and worked through the war years.

He lived with the Twigg family into his early teens and went to the local school, leaving just before the end of the war, aged fourteen, with no qualifications and few prospects. He worked on local farms, being strong and willing and there being a shortage of young men with so many away at the war. He helped with a milk round, dropping pints on doorsteps in the villages around Ashbourne. His first pay packet consisted of seventeen shillings and six pence, knowing Dad, he probably managed to save most of this.

Earning money here and there, over time he got enough together to make a start on his life as a farmer. Always enterprising, he begged the use of a small stable on the Twigg's farm and saved his money to buy a pregnant sow, some feed and some straw. He fed her on kitchen scraps and windfalls. Mother produced a healthy litter of piglets and just like that, he was in the pig business, a farmer.

His life around animals started early; as a kid, he had learned to ride and had ridden other people's horses to success at local showjumping events. He had a big bag of certificates and rosettes, in the big roll-top desk in the office, but he never took them out. I found them once and started to lay them out by colour on the office floor. The red ones were for first place. When he saw me, he made me put them back in the drawer. He seemed flushed with embarrassment rather than pride. He was determined to hide his past and hurried me up as I stuffed the ribbons back into the carrier bag. Now I felt guilty and confused as to why they were hidden and why success was a bad thing. I still got them out to have another look on a few occasions. As far as I know, they were still in the desk drawer when he died.

Perhaps shouting about his success as a horseman would have been boastful or 'brussen' as he (and absolutely no one else) called it. Brussen is a word that has a very specific meaning but which needs several other words to explain, which is of course what makes it a superb word. The words that almost describe it are: macho, full of bravado, possessed of a mistaken sense of superiority. He had a few useful words like brussen. It meant that he could get away with using the fewest words possible. He had no time for anyone who was brussen. They were big-heads in his book.

As we grew, he was keen for his sons to ride horses too, and when he had the money, a horse called Whiskey was bought. With my blond hair and little round National Health glasses, I was a dead ringer for the Milky Bar Kid; I even had a small Stetson and a holster with a silver pistol. But, sitting nervously on this animal, it seemed a long, long way to the ground.

When he came to us, Whiskey was young, strong and daft, prone to jumping over walls and heading off into the far distance. Despite only being twelve hands high, he seemed to be able to jump at least his own height and could clear a drystone wall with ease. When he escaped, as he often did, we would walk for miles to find him. Again, Dad had a sixth sense as to where he might be, usually with some other horses, having a high old time. Eventually, sick of Whiskey's adventures, Dad tied a big old tractor tyre to a long rope and secured it around the horse's neck with a wide collar. This slowed him down and made sure he stayed on our side of the walls around his field.

Initially, Whiskey was impossible to catch, but the tractor tyre made it easier to put a halter on him and, with this, a long rein. On the rein, Dad schooled this wild animal, running him round and round in circles until they were both worn out. Then a saddle was introduced, and after that, eventually, a very uncomfortable small boy would be placed carefully on his back, to go around in more circles until Whiskey got used to the idea. To the small boy, this seat was far from comfortable and the saddle rubbed against bare legs. Moving faster than a walk seemed recklessly fast, and the jiggling from a trot shook feet from stirrups and detached bottoms from saddles, resulting in horse and rider parting company, much to Dad's annoyance.

Eventually, sometimes, we were able to ride this beautiful animal quietly and without drama. We learned along with the horse and a rising trot soon started to show horse and rider in some kind of rough harmony. We even dared a canter every now and then. This schooling process was called 'breaking a horse in'. Whiskey was never properly broken; he always remained headstrong and wilful. But in Dad's hands, he was a lamb. Dad would ride him bareback, leaning back, his strong legs gripping the horse's sides, perfectly balanced, with no bridle or bit, just a halter and a handful of mane to hold on to. In the hands of a nervous and inexperienced rider though, the horse was liable to do pretty much as he pleased. Dad implored us to show the horse who was boss. Whiskey knew already.

Eventually, Whiskey was sold and replaced with another grey

named Dawn Boy, a much older, calmer, fatter and slower proposition. I was the only one who rode with any regularity and quite enjoyed sitting up high, although my skill levels and a complete lack of courage meant that jumping anything higher than a lolly stick was out of the question.

Dawn Boy was always hungry, and when being ridden out, he would sense we were turning for home and that it would be feeding time soon. On occasion, he simply could not wait and would set off at high speed, homewards, with me hanging on for dear life, pulling hard on the reins but having no slowing effect at all. Usually, I would be dumped on the floor and Dawn Boy would head for home. He was always easy to locate as his nose would be buried in the deepest, lushest patch of grass he could find. After a few experiences like that, I was pretty much done with horses.

Apart from dogs and horses, Dad was never sentimental about animals. When no longer productive, they would be despatched. None were given names, not even a house cow who was with us for years and years. She was a wonderfully gentle natured Jersey cow who gave us rich and creamy milk twice a day. Not a cow that lived in the house, as one of my kids imagined.

Nevertheless, Dad cared deeply about his livestock. All his senses were employed to ensure the welfare of his animals. He had an innate feel for when an animal was unwell. He could lean on a gate looking over a field of sheep grazing quietly and pick out the one that might, next day, be lying on its back with its feet in the air, what he called as 'dead as a nit'. Just by looking, he would see how it stood apart or how its head was bowed, or how it was slow to its feet. He would fetch the bottle of milky white penicillin solution and his big syringe to give it a shot that might just save its life.

In a barn full of cattle, he could identify any that were off colour by the quality of the snot and dribble coming from their noses and mouths. The health of a calf could be judged from the colour, quantity and consistency of what emerged from its rear end. Bright yellow was not good. He would move quietly among his animals, and calmly run his hand gently along their hides. Healthy cattle have bright shiny coats, soft to the touch, glossy and almost silky. The poorly one's skins were dry and coarse and rough. Their muscles would shudder when touched, as if cold. He could tell from their eyes or just by the way they carried themselves which ones were not doing well. At feeding time, they kept themselves apart from the others: hunched, withdrawn, miserable, shrinking into the dark corners of the barn.

He would devote many hours to saving his animals if they were ill, sitting with cows that had gone off their feet with milk fever, propping them up and surrounding them with straw bales so that if they did get up, but staggered again, and fell, they would fall on to something softer than the hard floor. He would hold an intravenous drip to replace the calcium needed to revive them, hoping they were going to get up and making sure they were steady when they did.

If he felt that the recovery prospects of a sick animal were slim, he would certainly be in favour of dispatching it to the abattoir before it could up sticks and die. Missing vital signs or just getting his timing wrong meant a visit from the knacker man from the local hunt kennels. He would bring his captive bolt gun and a winch to pull the still warm carcass into the back of his bloody truck, and Dad would receive pennies from the hunt, rather than pounds for the beef. Despair and resignation would be etched on his face if he lost a cow or if a calf was born dead. The difference between farming survival and ruin in the Pennine foothills were the many small events like these. All his stockman's skills were employed out of economic necessity.

Before ultra-sound pregnancy diagnosis, knowing whether a ewe was in lamb, a pig carrying a litter, or a cow a healthy calf, involved quiet examination and keen observation. He would know where to push and gently probe the mother's sides to feel what was going on. 'Knocking up the calf,' he called it, giving the little one a gentle nudge and feeling the calf recoil or wriggle would tell him all he needed to know. By observing how a ewe carried herself he could tell when it was time to move to the lambing shed. If a quiet descended on a sow and she started to use her bedding to make a large sow-shaped nest, piling up the sawdust and straw around her with soft snuffling grunts, he knew it was time.

A calf or a litter on the way meant he could afford to feed the mother for a few months more. A failure to get a cow in calf meant delay until she started to give more valuable milk. Repeated failures meant it was time for market or the slaughterhouse.

At birthing time, his instincts told him if a mother was

struggling with a labour, if perhaps a helping hand was needed to align a calf presenting the wrong way, or if the calf was just large and extra muscles were needed to bring it into the world. A long arm would be soaped up and extended into the birthing canal and Dad would have a feel around, his sense of touch working overtime as he tried to determine why the birth was just not happening. Was the calf even alive? He would feel the calf, working out how it lay, where its back and front legs were pointing and, from the contractions, how strong the cow was after hours in labour. If the calf was not presenting well, he might try and gently move a leg, only for the calf to move it back again. At least he knew it was still alive, deep inside its mother's womb and that patience would be required.

At times, more help was needed and lengths of rope with loops on the end would be passed around the legs of the calf and, working with the cows' contractions, a gentle pull was offered. Sometimes the ropes might need to be attached to a T-shaped ratchet device that exacted a constant pulling force. This could take hours, often in the dead of night. But a calf born alive, and a mother able to rest and recuperate from what must have been a traumatic experience, was an adequate reward.

A difficult birth was exhausting for both animal and farmer. On cold nights, the poor lighting in the cowsheds made the chill seem to cling. But to lose a cow and calf, would be economically unthinkable, so slowly, the calf would be introduced to the world. Bit by bit it might appear and then all at once in one agonising rush. The calf, often as groggy as the mother from the effort, would be dragged towards its mother's head, where the cow's large, rough tongue would massage life into rubbery limbs.

After a while – slowly – the calf would raise itself, often only as far as its front knees at first, then a back leg might be engaged before, still on its knees, it would steady itself, all the time with urgent licks from its mother. Dad might raise it onto its legs and hold it steady whist it swayed from side to side, getting used to its own weight, using its large and heavy head as a counterbalance, its legs straight, not daring to bend them for fear they might buckle. Gently, Dad would nudge it towards the cow's udder, placing the nearest teat in its hungry mouth, standing, waiting patiently, until it got the hang of it and the rich milk, heavy with colostrum and vital goodness, started to flow.

Come the morning, sometimes only a couple of hours later, the calf, fortified with the wholesome first milk, would have its head buried deep under its mother's belly, gently butting her udder to make the milk flow more readily, its stumpy tail flicking excitedly from side to side as it drank deeply. Later, it might be curled up asleep in the straw at its mother's feet as both rested, the cow breathing peacefully, deeply and rhythmically.

Later on, the family moved to a bigger farm, Greetham Lodge, which supported a large flock of sheep for a while and lambing time meant the ewes were brought closer to home and that all Dad's powers of observation were brought into play. Animals visibly labouring would be brought into the lambing shed and placed in individual pens to be watched over. If a mother was slow to lamb and needed a helping hand, this would be quickly administered, a muscular forearm inserted and the lambs removed – hopefully feet first, but sometimes backwards. The shock of the chill of the shed compared to the warmth of the womb would send a shudder through the whole body of this new small animal as it struggled to its feet

Dad would move from pen to pen. Newborn lambs would have the afterbirth and mucus cleared from snuffling noses before being placed where the mother could see them to let the bonding process begin. If a lamb was slow to revive from the shock of birth, he would give it a quick massage, a vigorous rub to stimulate its tiny energy. A newborn's natural instinct was to find a milky teat as soon as it was able to stand, and lambs would blindly prod their mothers' sides, looking for the vital source of rich colostrum. Dad would gently guide the animals in the right direction.

Once the lambs were up and drinking well, they would be marked with the same number as the mother so that in the chaos of moving mothers and their young out of the lambing shed and into the fields, the new family did not get separated. In the fields, close to the house, mothers would call out and lambs would skitter to their sides, bleating loudly back as they came. A newborn quickly learned the sound of their mother's voice and was able to pick their mum out from the cacophony of noise as dozens of mothers and hundreds of lambs were moved from barn to field.

Lambing time required long hours, vigilance and stamina, the whole team taking it in turns to watch over the activity in the lambing shed around the clock. Mothers might deliver three lambs, but as sheep's udders only have two teats, the smallest or weakest might not get the milk it needed to thrive. A process of adoption would need to start. A younger ewe may only have a single lamb and would therefore have too much milk. But mothers would naturally reject lambs that were not their own. They had to be introduced carefully, perhaps given the lamb the foster mother's smell to trick her into thinking the lamb was hers. Most of the time, this was successful, but some years, Mum had a posse of bottle-fed orphans in a small paddock at the end of the house who were quick to cry out if their feeding time was late and drank greedily from the bottles of warm formula milk that Mum made up.

The art of the stockman was employed at both ends of an animal's life. Farming was, after all, about the production of food, so Dad knew when a beast was ready for market by laying a hand on its back, feeling and sensing the quality of the flesh and just the right covering of fat to make the best eating. He would lay both hands on the back of a pork pig, assessing the strength and depth of the muscles that would become pork chops.

At Scout Dike, pork pigs, which had to be a certain weight to be accepted by the abattoir, were run through pig-sized weighing scales, their progress being recorded from week to week as Dad carefully calculated the rate at which the animals were growing compared to the amount of food they were given. This vital rate of conversion was the difference between profit and loss, and it led Dad to make changes to feed over time to boost growth.

He also selected the breeds of animal that best converted food to muscle meat, or that delivered a carcass with better confirmation. A solidly muscled beef animal would produce more saleable joints of topside, and pigs with longer bodies produced more chops. All these skills were self-taught, picked up by trial and error, and a keen instinct.

He could appraise a field of beef cattle and would know what they might look like on the hook, whether the flesh would be well covered in the fat that delivered the important flavour, how the rump, topside and silverside would cut up or if they had been 'done too well', meaning got too fat, and needed to be moved to leaner pastures to be properly ready for the butcher's block.

At the Ministry of Agriculture, before he was making a living out of livestock, Dad handed out subsidy to cattle farmers based on the quality of their stock. Then he would come home to his own cattle, applying exacting standards and proud of the animals he had reared from calves to be healthy and strong.

At dusk, in summer, his herd grazing quietly in the fields as the sun set, he might walk among the cattle, trailing a couple of boys with him. The dew might already be on the grass and the first chill of evening starting to fall. The animals would come to his call and crowd gently around us, nudging for attention, eating a fistful of sweet grass out of a hand, nibbling at Dad's jacket, never rushed, never urgent, no sharp movements, the beasts' rheumy breath filling the air, the constant buzz of flies all around. They sensed his calm and were calm too. He would talk gently to them, perhaps tapping one on the nose if they nudged too hard. His confidence around animals was imparted to his sons on these evenings and they became treasured moments when Dad might properly be at peace. Few words were spoken, just quiet harmony between stockman and stock.

He had an affinity for animals that was sometimes lacking in his human relationships. His stock trusted him, and he trusted his animals in a way that he never could bring himself to trust a human being. It was as if his animals lack of complication soothed him. He understood their simple needs for shelter and food, and they didn't answer back. To him, human needs were too complex. He had a genuine warmth around his livestock in a way that surfaced only fleetingly in the company of men and women. He was innately suspicious and questioning of human motives, and lived by the strict rule that you should never ever tell anyone your business. His animals never had ulterior motives. To be in his company was always easiest when he was around the farm, going about his work. This was his comfortable place. Elsewhere, he could be awkward, shy and reserved.

Above all, he understood that if he looked after his stock, they would look after him, that healthy and happy animals were profitable ones.

5

OUR MUM

Mum whistled all the time. I am sure she was doing it without thinking. There never seemed to be a discernible tune, but what tune there was, repeated, all day, according to Dad. She whistled while she worked. And she was always working.

I was only seven when Andrew was born, so with the four of us she had a full-time job. We had moved to a tiny bungalow in the village of Hoylandswaine by this point, and Dad was busy building his new farm at Scout Dike. After the farm buildings came the house. He mostly built that too, so he wasn't around much.

Mum had farming in her blood. She understood the seasons and the cycles of an agricultural life very well. She went to agricultural college where she studied dairying, before taking a job with the Ministry of Agriculture. Her first job was based in Huddersfield, from where she would travel around the Pennine hills, visiting the farms.

Nevertheless, starting married life with my father must have been quite different to how she had been brought up. Her father was a prosperous 'gentleman farmer'. He farmed a more hospitable hundred acres or so on the outskirts of a Nottinghamshire pit village, where he kept a herd of pedigree British Friesian cattle.

His approach to farming was quite different from that employed by my father, who, at least when he was starting out, could not afford the ample labour or new equipment that Grandad's farm had. Mum and Dad's way of farming was by necessity, altogether more hard graft, driven by the location on the edge of the moors and the lack of money. From the beginning, just making a living was hard. But Mum bought into this without question; she shared the vision, she aspired to the life of the wife of a farmer, and Dad was the one she chose. Her time travelling from farm to farm in the hills outside Huddersfield meant she had no misapprehensions as to how hard farming could be in the area.

Mum worked with a cheerfulness and resolve that belied the shortage of money, a constant and irresistible force, a foundation stone for the family and my father's rock. She allowed him to dream and to invest every penny they had in the farm.

She did everything for her growing family. The house was clean and tidy. She made our beds, picked up our clothes where they were dropped, washed them, and even ironed our socks. She cleaned behind our ears, giving two small boys a bath at the same time to save on hot water. She put plasters on skinned knees and toothpaste on our brushes so we didn't use too much. She cut the ends off the toothpaste tubes to make sure we got every last bit out, and told us that three sheets of loo roll was all that was needed! She forced cod-liver oil down our throats every night but followed it up with a spoonful of sweet rose-hip syrup to take the taste away. When we were ill, she was ever ready with the kaolin and morphine mix or the junior disprin.

Mostly though, in those early years, she scrimped and she saved and she scrimped some more to make the money go further, saving up for the farm Dad was building. At the end of a long day, this meant sitting by the fire, rifling through her work bag to find strands of wool of the right colour for darning our socks, or working her sewing machine to make clothes for us to go to school in.

She must have despaired of us all at times, going out neat and tidy, scrubbed and with hair neatly brushed, but coming back mucky, usually covered in something unspeakable from the cowshed. She once made me a new pair of trousers. I promptly fell over, skinning a knee and making a big hole. She hid her upset and dismay well. There was no money for more new trousers, so out came the sewing machine and neat patches were sewn into the holes.

Mum was from a well-spoken family and she tried hard to get us to speak in the same way. She was not pushing at an open door, but she was largely successful in 'learning us to speak proper'. Years later, we all have a few traces of our Yorkshire roots. I still say grass, never grarse, and a castle is absolutely

37

not and never can be called a carstle. My brothers and I – much to Mum's despair – would automatically switch to broad Yorkshire when in each other's company. My 'brothers' voice was the one I used at school, just to fit in. Posh kids were few and far between and not taken kindly to. But around Mum, we all spoke nicely.

Mum provided three cooked meals a day, every day. Having started early, a full cooked breakfast was what Dad required: bacon, eggs, sausages and fried bread, sometimes a bit of fried liver or kidneys, and maybe a few mushrooms if he had spotted any on his walk down the fields to bring the cows in to milk. We all joined him in this meaty start to the day.

Lunch would be meat and at least two veg most days. Dad would complain if it fell short of this benchmark. Always in a hurry, he needed dinner (as he insisted on calling the midday meal) at the given time and would chivvy Mum along if it was even five minutes late. He would eat so fast and clear the plates from in front of any laggards, depositing them on the draining board as he stepped back into his boots and pulled on his coat and flat cap, half out the door already. He said, 'first fed, best fed' and so we too would rip into the food as if we hadn't eaten for days. There was never anything left uneaten on the sides of the plate, which would have been unforgivable in my parents' eyes. There was nothing we didn't like. We did not grow up picky, or faddy as Dad called it: everything on the table was eaten.

Mum would make a cake most days. Cake never lasted two whole days, even a big one. She looked with disdain on anyone who ate what she called 'bought cake', the inferior stuff from the shops. So, every day there would be huge Victoria sponges with butter icing and strawberry jam, or rich chocolate cakes with cocoa in the butter icing. All would be wolfed down with tea at elevenses, or at tea-time, just before evening milking. Never mind that we had eaten a full dinner only two hours before. There would always be toast and home-made marmalade; she would take us along the farm lanes, picking blackberries for jam, and we would stir the jam pan for her, standing on a chair by the stove.

When the cakes were in the oven, filling the house with a rich sweetness, we loved to lick the spoons and clean out the bowls with a spatula until not a trace of mixture was left. Competition for this job was fierce. The creamy, un-cooked cake mix, with crunchy sugar, was easily as delicious as the finished article. The only exception to the 'bought cake' rule was a Battenberg, a vivid block of yellow and pink with a darker yellow marzipan outside, the colours so bright they lit up the kitchen. Dad had a sweet tooth and would bring one home from his travels for the Ministry, presenting it as a great gift. With a degree of reverence and wonder, it would be thinly sliced for a maximum number of servings, even lasting two days sometimes.

Home-made cakes needed home-made butter. We always had pools of fresh-off-the-farm milk. Mum would let it settle, the rich cream rising to the top in the cool of the larder. She would skim off the cream with a flat pan, with holes in for the milk to drain away, conjuring up huge lumps of rich butter which she would fashion into blocks with two wooden butter pats that looked like rectangular table tennis bats. The butter was slightly salty and coloured the deepest rich yellow. Mum would make a pattern on top.

The dairy cows provided endless unpasteurised milk for a thirsty family. Mum would swear by the goodness in this unprocessed nectar, telling us how healthy. big and strong we would grow if we drank it all up. She was never ill and claimed it was the untreated milk that kept her healthy.

She had a big white enamel bowl with a jug to match, from an old washstand. She would fill the bowl with fresh milk and add in a pot of natural 'live' yogurt and pop it in the airing cupboard with a tea towel on top, presumably to stop stray socks falling in. After a couple of days of incubation, we would have gallons of yogurt, tart and fresh, with huge strawberries floating on top.

I preferred the smell of a freshly baked cake to the reek of the fermenting milk in the cupboard at the top of the stairs, but yogurt was from another place altogether. Slightly continental, European, maybe a bit Scandinavian. So exotic that nobody knew for certain how to spell it. Was it joghurt, joghourt, yoghourt or just plain yogurt?

In our early years, she brought us up on a tight budget and a frugality born of post-war rationing that lasted with her all her life. Nothing went to waste. Leftovers were made into something else. Any peelings or scraps were stored in a bucket and fed to the animals.

We were never extravagant. A treat would be a Mars bar, once in a blue moon. This would be carefully cut into slices, one for each of us. Mars bars seemed bigger in those days. The broken chocolate crumbs left on the chopping board would be carefully picked up and savoured too.

The other luxury we looked forward to was the visit of the 'Pop Man', who would come round once a fortnight with big bottles of fizzy pop – dandelion and burdock, or sarsaparilla – both absolutely disgusting, but Dad liked them. For us there was cream soda, bright pink with a white froth. The Pop Man would drop off the big bottles and take away the empties.

Mum's frugal approach came to the fore at Sunday tea. In summer this would consist of a single tin of John West red salmon which as the family grew would somehow be made to go around all of us. We had a huge plate of salad, always iceberg lettuce, tomatoes and cucumber, nothing as exotic as a radish, unless she had some ready in the garden, and piles of white sliced bread and thinly spread home-made butter. No matter how plentiful Mum's butter was, it still had to be used with care. So the butter would be scraped on and scraped back off again.

Heinz Salad Cream would accompany all this. It had to be Heinz – no others would do. Mum and I would pick at the salad until it was all gone. John was always a salad dodger. This would be followed by a tin of some fruit from the warm places on the planet. Del Monte pineapple rings in light sugar syrup from Latin America, Bartlett pears, huge, peeled and halved, all the way from Australia, cling peach segments or

41

a tin of bright orange mandarins. Heaven. These would, of course, be eaten with even more bread and butter as the family banter flowed. We would happily gather around the table, for a change, in no rush to be getting on. Even Dad would relax, his work done for the week.

With Mum in the bungalow looking after the family, Dad was able to work on developing the farm and making a start on the house there. He already had some animals at the new place and was starting to build up the numbers. Progress was slow, a result of not enough hours in the day and not enough money to go round.

All her life, Mum brought a sense of stability and constancy; she was our anchor, with a matter-of-fact acceptance of everything that life could throw at her. I do not recall her complaining until she was very old and her failing mobility started to slow her down. As we were growing up, she accepted that together, she and Dad were building a future that involved sacrifice and hard work. If she ever questioned Dad's dreams, we never heard it. They never had rows or even raised their voices to one another, and I can never remember tears from my mother, or father for that matter, no matter how frustrating the lack of money must have made life at times. Self-pity never raised its ugly head, and emotions were always kept firmly in check.

If her resolve ever slackened, it was never apparent. . While Dad was quick to temper, the cause was usually some inanimate object and over in seconds; Mum never lost hers. Any hopes and dreams of her own were set aside so that the dreams they shared together could be achieved. She took pleasure in her sons, and was proud of the things we achieved, of the stable platform she had helped to build for us and the appetite for hard work that was her second nature and which she shared with all of us.

6

SCOUT DIKE

Scout Dike was where Mum and Dad built their dream. Years of saving up had enabled Dad to buy a bit of land to call his own, no more than twenty acres, on the slope leading down to the river, the Scout Dike. Here he would build his model farm.

The river, a tributary of the Don, tumbled down the steep steps of the reservoir over-flow higher up the valley before running through our land. The Dam was the largest of a series, holding back the water that spilled from the moors, and provided the drinking water for the small towns that followed the course of the Don down towards Sheffield.

We had four fields, all down to permanent pasture and ringed by solid drystone walls. But Mum and Dad owned it and planned to build the farm, with a house next to it, perched on a terrace above the stream.

The breeze-block farm buildings were taking shape, as fast as Dad could afford to build. Mostly, he did everything himself. A large rectangle consisted of sow stalls, loose boxes, a feed store, farrowing pens and fattening pens for the older pigs. He had no training as a builder but applied common sense, a spirit level and a plumb line, and learned fast from the tradesmen he brought in when he could afford it. The buildings were designed so that everything sloped slightly down the hill, so all the effluent, carried by gravity, could be collected in large tanks, before being spread on the land. My dad was clever like that.

From the little bungalow at Greenside, we would go to the farm as often as possible. Our job was often to keep the cement mixer busy, shovelling in piles of sand, pebbles and Blue Circle cement, splashing in enough water to make the mix runny and moving it by barrow to the latest building site. The thickness had to be just right. We became fit and strong and tanned and tired! The concrete would be levelled and then, with me at one end of a plank of wood and Dad at the other, the concrete would be tapped down to make the floor of the building. It was back-breaking work.

We worked hard, and while we did, Dad would impart his wisdom, always by example rather than with words. Things like, always fill your barrow from the low end, so you don't need to lift stuff up so high, or never move stuff twice if you don't have to, or make sure the barrow is facing in the right direction, so you don't have to turn round when it is full and heavy. All decent metaphors for life.

As soon as the buildings were ready (sometimes, in his urgency, before), he began to stock them with animals. Fortunately, pigs multiply quickly. Soon, we were building and laying new concrete as fast as we could, to keep up with the growing numbers.

In the front field, which sloped from the river up to the road, our pony shared the grazing with our gentle, patient house cow. She would amble to the shallow river crossing, under the tree house, ready to be milked, and whoever was up for the milking job would bring her into the buildings for a feed of corn which would make her stand still long enough for milking.

She was milked by hand, an unpleasantly hot, fly-blown and sweaty job in summer. As she swished her tail from side to side to swoosh the flies away, she would catch you full in the face with her heavy, shit-matted switch. In winter, milking was a warming job, as the milker on a low stool with a bucket between the knees, rested his head on the gently heaving belly and reached down to the warm udder to squeeze the milk out. It made a satisfying rhythmic sploosh, gurgling as the bucket filled with hot, frothy, full-cream Jersey milk. Our townie next door neighbour was hardly able to believe that this was where milk came from. He thought it came in a bottle from the Co-op milkman every morning.

My father had a deep well of self-confidence, although he was never brussen! He had an inbuilt belief in his own abilities to tackle pretty much anything, a can-do attitude that would have him figure things out and, through trial and some error, things would get done. It was almost deciding first to commit, and then to figure out how.

It had been with this confident resourcefulness that he went into farming, persuading the landlords to let Top of the Town Farm to him over many more experienced and better qualified candidates. It was how he went about building the farm at Scout Dike, the house that was to sit beside it and then a successful farm shop, long before farm shops became commonplace. He had no experience of any of these things really; he had never built a new barn, or designed and built a house or run a retail business.

Driven by the need to make progress, he asked more of the world, trying to shape it into what he wanted it to be. Sometimes out of economic necessity, he just watched and learned and made a little knowledge go a long way. He would stitch together the knowledge he acquired and put it to good use. It seemed that the hours spent quietly working away, thinking things through in the most minute detail, had enabled his vision to form in his mind's eye, almost down to the last breeze block.

Dad continued to juggle his work with the ministry for a while. But every other hour was devoted to the farm at Scout Dike, where the livestock continued to increase in number, requiring his attention morning and night, along with the constant laying of more and more concrete and the addition of more buildings. The faster he could build the farm up and the faster it could be made profitable, the faster he could drop his job and become a full-time farmer.

The expansion of the farm meant that our own land was not enough to feed all of the animals. So, in exchange for as much pig-slurry as they needed, our neighbours were more than willing to let us graze our stock on their ample grass.

One such neighbour was Kelly, who had a scruffy little farm at the top of the hill in front of Scout Dike. He milked a few cows, never seemingly enough to provide him with much of an income, and consequently his farm stayed scruffy; broken-down tractors and discarded bits of farm machinery were left where they were parked to rust gently in the wind and rain, nettles growing up in clumps of ever-increasing size around abandoned machines that had been long stripped for useful parts.

Kelly was about as tall as he was round, a pugnacious little man with two neatly tended patches of hair on either side of his head and absolutely nothing on the top. His mouth was perpetually open, as if the word 'Eh?' would come out of it any moment. His eyes were narrow and his chin tilted up, permanently asking a question. He seemed to be in a bad temper, all the time. His trousers, held up with baler twine, sagged beneath an ample belly, and he fidgeted constantly, tugging them up, a mess of nervous ticks and twitches.

He was very fond of swearing. A lot. This meant that if Kelly came to visit, usually to borrow a piece of equipment, because he had broken something of his own, we would be shepherded out of earshot to make sure that we didn't learn any more new words to add to the ones we heard the last time he'd visited.

Perhaps because Dad thought that Kelly didn't look after his bony cows particularly well, or maybe because Kelly always had a cigarette glued to his bottom lip, or perhaps just because he liked a beer, Kelly was not held in high regard. But even Dad admitted that he had his uses.

Getting our beasts back from Kelly's fields was always a harum-scarum challenge as it involved crossing the main Sheffield to Huddersfield road. We would usually move thirty to forty animals at a time. This number meant perfecting the art of being in at least two places at once. Kelly was no help at all: not fast enough on his feet, he would simply make sure our cattle didn't invade his yard. He would block his gate, swearing loudly.

Dad was not quite as speedy as he used to be either, and that meant that he would usually be the one bringing up the rear, with John and me up front diverting the young stock, hopefully in the direction we wanted them to go without being run over by the traffic on the main road.

The cattle would be run out of the field and onto Kelly's lane, which led directly onto the main road. John and I would go ahead to make sure that the various gates off Kelly's lane were closed and that some poor unsuspecting neighbour of Kelly's did not get their front lawn comprehensively trampled. Meanwhile, I would be running full tilt to position myself in the middle of the main road, arms waving like a mad man, trying to slow the traffic, ahead of the imminent arrival of the cattle, now moving at a canter.

We had to make sure that they turned right and then almost immediately left, which meant that one of us had to attempt to overtake and loop around to divert the herd, virtually impossible to do as by now, they were building up speed. Meanwhile, Dad would be bawling instructions at the top of his voice and Kelly would be cursing loudly. We could not possibly hear properly because we were running so fast to get ahead of the cattle.

We always hoped that they would tire before we did, perhaps spot a bit of fresh grass that was just too tempting, allowing us to get our breath back, but that was wishful thinking. Eventually we would turn them into our field and they would dance and skip, heels kicking skyward, through the new pasture and down to the river. Exhausted and breathless we would lean, both arms on the top of the gate, chests heaving with the effort. Dad would have caught up by now, asking us why we'd let them get away from us. Again.

As well as the farm buildings, he also made a start on building the house that we were to move to when it was finished. A level platform was cut into the hillside and trenches were dug for the foundations, the outline of the outside walls and each room already clear. The trenches were filled with concrete. Dad had been forced by the local planners to get some proper drawings made for the build and he would pore over these, hand rubbing the back of his sun-browned neck, before taking his long tape measure and checking, again and again, where the openings for the doors were meant to be. He sucked his bottom lip as he wandered around with his spirit level, perhaps baffled how cement, laid level, could be so far from level when dried. But slowly the block interior walls and brick outer walls took shape, corners first, then around the door ways, under the windows up to sill height. Dad worked late into the night, moving blocks and bricks to the places they were needed, so the bricklayer, if Dad could afford to employ one for a few days, would be able to start the next morning.

Scaffolding was brought for the upstairs rooms and the roof trusses were lifted into place with the loader on the front of a tractor; ropes were used to get them upright. All this was done as fast as could be afforded. But soon a handsome, red-brick, four-bedroomed house emerged from the rubble of the building site.

Dad turned his hand to building cupboards, the electrics and the plumbing, and plasterers were employed before Mum undertook the not inconsiderable job of adding several coats of paint. We moved in long before the house was finished and for the first few years, we had no central heating. The Big Lads shared a bedroom and the Little Lads had their own room too. The kitchen had a split stable-style door that opened out to the fields and the river and the farmyard and an adventure playground for me, my brothers and our friends.

The Ward family moved in next door to us at Scout Dike as it was being built. We pronounced their name, as they did, Waard. The family became the Waardy's. It consisted of John, who ran a steel fabrication business, a wife who drove a little sports car and wore very big sunglasses, all the time, and three boys about our age.

51

The Waard boys versus the Kirby boys was a permanent fixture at pretty much any sport you could mention. We loved motorbikes and they would bring theirs to ride round our fields. We would also play football on the front lawn, and there were Speedway matches. We would throw sand on our drive and speed up and down. If they lost, which they usually did, one or several of them would leave for home in tears.

As we grew, motorbikes became a permanent part of our weekends. I had a motocross bike, as did John. Unfortunately, loud motocross bikes were not at all compatible with the horses, and we badly needed the steeply banked and bumpy field where the horses grazed for our scramble track. So the horses had to go and Dad reluctantly sold them.

On Sunday afternoons, along with the Waardy boys, we would load the bikes into the cattle trailer and head to a motocross circuit not far from home. We would blast around the track until we fell off or all the bikes broke or both, and we had to come home. Too often I would end up falling in a gorse bush and come out covered in prickles, cut and bruised. John was far more skilful than me, and even though his bike had a smaller engine, he could beat me hands down – probably because I was scared witless.

At Scout Dike, we grew as the buildings and the house that we were all to regard as 'home' grew with us.

7

GREENSIDE

Number 17 Greenside, where we lived while the house at Scout Dike was being built, was a small bungalow, one of a long line of identical bungalows. This was the first house that they owned; the farm had been rented. Here, my brothers Sam and Andrew were born. They were forever now to be called the Little Lads. John and I were the Big Lads, a classification that Mum continued to use for the rest of her life.

It was a neat, square building with a strip of grass at the front, overlooked by a huge picture window, a square lawn at the back, and a garage attached to one side, behind which my abundant crops of rhubarb and garden mint grew, watered regularly by small boys who couldn't be bothered to go into the house for a wee.

Number 17 looked across the road, down the road and up the road to other bungalows, all the same. Coming home, up the hill, in the car, we would chant 'that's not it – that's not it' as we passed each house, before arriving at our one, three houses from the top, and shouting out, 'That's it!'

Standing at the top of our road, looking south, the countryside dipped steeply down to Guyder Bottom, where my mate Andy's dad had a smallholding with a few sheep and chickens and rabbits raised for the pot. Their house was close to an abandoned mine shaft. Reading *Adventures of Huckleberry Finn* at school provided plenty of fuel for our fertile imaginations. Who knew what horror might be walled up in this old mine, and on visits to Andy's house the old workings acted like a magnet. We would push through the rusty fence and wade through the nettles and brambles that grew in profusion around the old workings. The buildings had been pulled down or were falling down all by themselves. There was never anyone around, but we still crept closer as silently as we were able, peering around corners and through the undergrowth to get a look at the rusty metal doors, barred and padlocked and hiding the entrance to the mine. We would get as close as we dared, half expecting to hear a scratching sound from some poor soul locked underground by mistake, or fearing discovery or that something might leap from the old workings and drag us all down into the depths.

With Andy and other school friends we would roam widely, either on our bikes or on foot. A lot of my mates were farmers' sons and there was always the call of jobs to be done. Andy had his own chickens and tended them at the end of each day. We might head over to see Charles 'Chopper' Stanley. His dad trained horses on their farm.

From Andy's place, the land rippled away into the distance with the outskirts of Barnsley visible on the furthest hill. The countryside was greener to the south, further away from the moors, with small fields surrounded by hedges and tall trees as far as the eye could see.

Following Hamper Lane, the track that ran parallel to our road, would take you to the top of the hill and views in the other direction, north towards Thurlstone and Penistone; at times, the land beyond the towns seemed to rear up at the sky. Clear days made the moors seem much closer, the big sky towering above. The evening sun, low in the sky, would cause the purple heather to shimmer. Cloud-shadows on the land passed quickly by. Low cloud made the hills seem distant, and the towns and villages dotted along the escarpment huddled in the lee of the hills behind.

Opposite our house lived my friend Simon. A few doors down was Nick, my friend for a while, until he chucked a piece of coal at me that split my forehead and needed stitches. After that, we weren't so friendly. We would play football in the road, with jumpers for goals. It was in Simon's garage that I first learned to ride a bike. I would mount up, bracing myself against the garage wall, and then let go, pedalling like mad, veering from side to side and out into the road, not daring to steer and only stopping in time to miss hitting the wall on the other side. Eventually, I managed to sprint out of Simon's drive and head up the hill. But my knees and elbows were constantly skinned and bloody, bruised, black and blue. Further down lived lovely blonde Karen with her lovely blonde mother – who I am sure Dad had a soft spot for.

Behind our house was a small coppice and we would clamber over the low stone wall and set up camp there, lighting small fires and trying to cook things on the end of sticks, or boil tin cans full of water. We always got bored long before the water boiled. We were far enough away to be left to our own devices, but close enough to hear Mum call us in for supper. Here we would set up traps for rabbits and make rope swings from whatever we could find. In summer, the leaves obscured us from adult view and girls were definitely not allowed.

At Greenside, the family grew. John and I had two annoying little brothers, too small to be of have any interest in the games we wanted to play. For a while, separated from the farm, we felt like normal kids, with a normal family life, no longer dictated by the timetables of the farming day. We had a mum that stayed at home and looked after us and a dad who went to work first thing and came back late. At weekends though, we would spend long days at the new farm and the building site that was to be our new house at Scout Dike.

8

A TIME OF DARKNESS

Whether Mum's indomitable spirit was acquired by proximity to my father, or perhaps it was something she was born with, she always took adversity in her stride. The numerous setbacks of a farming life were met with patience. But it was during the darkest days of the 1967 foot-and-mouth-disease outbreak that the steel at her core revealed itself.

As part of his work for the Ministry of Agriculture, Dad was called away for weeks on end, supervising the cull and the disposal of thousands and thousands of cattle, sheep and pigs in Shropshire and into the borderlands with Wales. Working desperately to stop the spread of the disease, entire herds were wiped out. Swathes of countryside had every animal killed, as the government tried to build a 'fire break' to halt, or at least slow down, the rapid spread of the pandemic. The life's work of farmers whose properties were infected, or simply just in the wrong place would be erased. For years afterwards, the fields would be bereft of cattle and sheep as though the countryside was still reeling from the shock.

Almost half a million animals had to be shot and buried or burned, the smoke from the fires, visible for miles, lasted for weeks, the acrid smell of burning flesh, hung in the air. I cannot imagine how Dad must have felt, overseeing this destruction. His heart must have wept for his fellow farmers. In typical fashion, this horror was never discussed. But my abiding memory of this time was of darkness and our parents' faces drawn with worry and fatigue.

It soon became apparent just how precarious things were. Dad was away full time. There was no foot-and-mouth on our side of the Pennines. The slaughter policy was working to contain the spread, but still more than two thousand farms were infected and their livestock destroyed. Dad was among this carnage all week, working long hours, living in hotels and only coming home for a snatched day or two at a time.

Foot-and-mouth is highly infectious and can be transmitted by several means. He could have been carrying the disease on his boots, on the wheels of his car, or on his clothes. The worry must have been unbearable. He was walking a tightrope. His employers at the ministry did not know about his farm and had they known he would have been dismissed without question, and the essential money that this 'proper job' provided would have ended.

Mum took over the running of the farm, keeping things going, feeding and bedding down before day light, organising what help she could, then getting John and me fed and ready for school. Andrew was only one and Sam not much older. Later, after school, she would be back to the farm to do it all again. There was no other choice. John and I 'helped' where we could; we were too small to be left at home alone. She worked all hours under unimaginable strain to keep things together while Dad was away.

Foot-and-mouth dominated the news. Maps were shown of its inexorable spread. Hundreds of farmers lost their life's work, hundreds of families lost everything. Foot-and-mouth never did spread to our side of the Pennines. Somehow Mum and Dad had got through this crisis, working together, as they always did, to make sure what needed doing was done.

9

GETTING ON

Communication was not Dad's greatest strength. His idea of a greeting was to look directly at you through narrowed eyes and raise his chin, almost imperceptibly: a slight jerking back of the head. One economical movement. It was not unfriendly, but not particularly friendly either, just an economy of movement, sometimes ambiguous, sometimes leaving the recipient of the 'greeting' in no doubt at all as to its meaning.

If you were a stranger, or an unwelcome visitor or for some reason were 'suspicious', which in Dad's mind probably included pretty much everyone, the upwards jerk of the head would be quick and slightly aggressive, the eyes narrower, lips thinner, accompanied by a furrowed-brow scowl as he quickly weighed you up, instantly sceptical that you might have anything useful for him. This was the visual equivalent of a tetchy, abrupt, 'What do you want?'

In his mind, pretty much everyone wanted something. He was

almost saying, 'Can't you see I'm busy?' I don't think it ever occurred to him that this was probably a bit rude. It was just how it was with people who interrupted his day and stopped him from getting on.

People he knew, even family, got the slower, more considered, softer featured, upward lift of the chin and perhaps a thin-lipped half smile. More welcoming perhaps, more open, the slightly more considered, softer movement of the head suggesting it might, just might, be OK to start a conversation. But the question in the gesture was pretty much the same, irrespective of the expression. There was never a 'Hello, how are you today?' or a 'What have you been up to?' or a 'You are looking well': no small talk, no open and welcoming invitation to have a chat. He didn't hold with chatting at all. He might not even break stride or pause to talk to you. This could intimidate most people, frankly, including those closely related to him.

This way, he shielded himself from the world, keeping it at arm's length, allowing in only the people and things that he was familiar with, on his terms. That, and he was always, always busy. When we moved to Greetham Lodge, the farm was down a long lane, standing away from the road, and protected by a five-bar gate, enough to dissuade idle enquiries and just the way he liked it.

He was a man of great reserve, very self-contained, capable of fun, and he had a wicked sense of humour that came out in practical jokes, but he always held a great deal back.

He would own up to only a few acquaintances and admit to

even fewer friends. But lonely was never something you could imagine him being. He was comfortable in his own company and he had his livestock, and he had his plans. Ideas burned inside him, driving him on. And he had his family. For us, he was ever-present, a relentless and irresistible force, from which we all took our lead when we were small, holding hands and walking alongside him. Then as we got older, most of the time, at least for me, it was a case of skittering to keep up, taking quick breathless steps and usually, awkwardly, standing in the wrong place, trying to not get in the way, as he went about his work.

The drive to be 'getting on' was ever present, in every minute of every waking hour, almost a deeply suppressed anger when his impatience spilled over into frustration. Perhaps this was the fuel that sustained him. There was always something that needed to be done, and done now, or at least very soon. As he gave shape to the farm at Scout Dike there was not only the need to house an ever-increasing number of animals, but also the pressing need to make money. At Greetham Lodge, the same profit motive drove him on. This made him hard to keep up with. That he was a workaholic was not in doubt, but he would have never defined himself as such. He was the work and the work was him.

When I left home, visits to the family were mainly to see Mum. Little or no concessions came from Dad. I might have driven for a couple of hours to be there, but all I would get would be a few words while he put his boots on and headed out the door. We might sit for half an hour while he had his lunch. Nothing was allowed to interrupt the farming timetable, dictated by milking the cows at both ends of the day, feeding round and bedding down, and then all the jobs in between.

On my increasingly infrequent visits, conversations between us were stilted and awkward through lack of practice, always snatched at as if on a timer. This never allowed for proper conversations, just a high-speed gabble through any news, followed by awkward silences where more in-depth conversations should have been. He wanted to know less and less about what the family were doing, just in case there were things he had to worry about, on top of all the things he already had on his mind. At mealtimes he would be clearing the table and dumping the plates on the side before everyone had finished, eager for relief from having to talk or just keen to get back to his jobs.

Sitting for lunch, he would ask me the same question every time: 'What are you busy with at the moment?' Being fully occupied was a virtue, the only way to be. On a farm it was a necessity. I am not sure he heard my answers, and am certain that if he did, he had no real perception of what being 'in marketing' meant. If we had problems, he didn't really want to hear them. Was he sure that he had provided us all with the resources we needed to sort things out for ourselves?

If I wanted to chat, I had to tag along while he got on with his work, always a pace behind, our staccato conversation fitting in with his constant motion as he moved cows in for milking or fed his calves. I would try to conjure up a discussion by observing that his cattle looked well, or that his latest building project was progressing nicely. He might even pause to point something out, but often I would be left stranded, wondering where best to stand so as not to get run over as he climbed up on a tractor. I was embarrassed that my lack of common sense was so clearly on show for him to see.

I never remember asking him for advice, or asking Mum for that matter. If I had a big decision to make, I made it myself. Advice was never spontaneously given. We all grew up just like them, making our own decisions, taking responsibility, making our own beds and lying in them.

John worked with Dad every day. The sometimes-repetitive routines of the day meant it was not necessary for them to communicate much, and it seemed to me that they just didn't in any sense of the word. Things were communicated by intuition. Jobs to do were obvious and if one of them saw something that needed to be done, they just did it. As my brothers and I grew, we had our jobs around the farm. These were assumed, rather than divided up through instruction. This usually meant that John or Andy did the tractor work. They were good at it. It just happened and was never planned; everyone just got on with their work.

Dad was driven by more than a long 'to-do' list. I think his impatience grew from the desire not to get ahead, but to catch up. Leaving school at fourteen, struggling then to read and write, had left him a long way behind – the word 'backward', so often applied to him when he was at school, had left him at the back of the pack. His progress was his way of telling the world that he was good enough. Chasing constantly to catch up made him restive, driven and obsessive, starting early every day, finishing late. He was defined by the progress he made.

He was undoubtedly dyslexic, but when he was at school dyslexia wasn't discussed or even diagnosed and he was labelled as 'thick', or slow. Both things he was not. The only book I remember him looking at, ever, was the *Reader's Digest Great World Atlas*. The only thing he read with any consistency was *Farmers Weekly* and the *Speedway Star* and I'm sure even then he only looked at the pictures. He gave his dyslexia to his sons. Over the years, we have come to regard this as a gift, because being labelled as thick at school – just like Dad – gave us all, by turns, his drive, energy and ambition to prove the world wrong.

Dad's childhood experiences had left him with an unhealthy disregard for schooling. His input into our own education was limited, and there were few words of encouragement. He might read my school report and give me a soppy-stern look of mock disapproval. He wanted us to work hard and any messing around at school was definitely frowned upon. His main threat was that if we didn't do well at school we would all end up as bin men when we grew up. Was he confident that the work ethic drummed into us from an early age would get us everything we wanted? Was he leading by example?

His energy was seemingly endless, but he was a slow engine with lots of torque, constant deliberate forward progress, powerful and irresistible but low-geared, grinding out the progress one job at a time. This way, Dad would pace himself through his long days.

His lack of qualifications belied his intelligence. He picked up practical skills simply by watching, trying, failing and trying again. Over the years, he taught himself farming, animal husbandry, building, electrical work, plumbing, carpentry, butchery, how to run a successful retail business and how to mend pretty much anything. These abilities gave him deep-seated confidence and a can-do approach. All my brothers inherited his practicality and common-sense skills.

Dad's assuredness rarely surfaced, never turned to hubris and he was never boastful. He was just quietly confident that, with application, stuff got done, progress could be made.

I think he was emotionally dependent on taking forward steps. I am sure that he must have been told how useless he was by his father or inconsiderate teachers, and he was determined to prove them wrong. He would tell us that unless you were going forwards, you were going backwards. This often meant that any money the farm made went immediately towards finishing the roof of a new barn, the frame of which might have stayed un-clad for months, waiting for the funds. Or it might mean another load of sand and cement and some more concrete to be mixed. Progress was measured by square meters of concrete laid. This meant we were always short of money, so finding economical ways to get things done became second nature.

He was a man who had few words for anyone, most of the time. If Mum had arranged to have friends over, there would be a lot of petulant moaning: 'Aw, do we have to do that tonight?' But when he was there, he would unfold, gradually at first, like the first hawthorn blossom, still a bit spiky underneath.

His approach to anything and everyone was usually guarded and suspicious. But sometimes, in company, he could confound us all by becoming almost chatty, quietly conspiratorial, intimate, genuinely funny, wry and full of stories. It was as if all that not-talking had enabled Dad to observe life's idiocies, to take in, to listen hard and store away stories just for this occasion.

10

UNTIL THE COWS COME HOME

When we lived at Top of the Town, some mornings I would step out of the steamy, range-warmed kitchen early, closing the door softly behind me. My feet would feel the chill of the stone-flag floor of the porch as I slipped my wellies on. Proper, black ones, like Dad's. I would pull my duffle coat around me and push my hands deep into the pockets.

'Have you wet the bed?' Dad might call, a broad grin on his face as he saw me, all purpose, heading out over the bottom yard early doors. I would ignore him but still feel that prickle of embarrassment. I had to be getting on with my jobs, now I was big. I would stride, workmanlike, over the uneven cobbles, grass poking miserably between the cold sandstone sets, leading to the lane and the steep slope up to the stack yard.

Lots of doors led off the bottom yard; Dad, busy already with the morning feeding round, would be working quickly in and out of each by turns, checking the animals, his practised eye quickly scanning to make sure all the stock were healthy. A large barn door opened to the dark recesses of the cowsheds, the calf pens and the feed stores. The single bulb, suspended with twine, dusty from the milled feed, gave off a sallow, yellow light. The shadows were deep and long and moved as the lightbulb swung in the draught from the open door.

The barn was a pungent place; the smell of urine stung the nostrils. Once used to it, the multiple smells of the feed store emerged: the sweetness of the sugar beet pulp, the bitter-beer smell of the fermenting brewers' grains and the heady-fresh fragrance of last summer's hay. The cattle, shuffling and murmuring softly from their stalls, poked their heads over and watched me pass. Noses snuffled through holes in loose box doors, scenting the morning and wondering where their breakfast was.

I would turn to head up the slope, under the lowering sky. The stack yard was to my left, the high drystone wall between our lane and the Smith's garden to my right. The twin piles of winter feed and bedding, one of hay bales and the other of straw, seemed so tall. A green tarpaulin on top of the stacks flapped gently in the wind.

Tractors and trailers were parked in the top yard. The massive red Massey-Harris and the smaller Fordson Major, bright blue with orange wheels. Both are ancient and require patience and no small mechanical skill to keep them going. But they were all that could be afforded at the start of Dad's farming journey. I was both terrified and fascinated by these big machines.

On cold mornings, Dad would bring them to life, spraying ether down the exhaust stacks to encourage them to fire up. Diesel fumes poured out as the engines turned slowly over before roaring to life with a fumy belch, the heady mixture of ether and diesel filling the chill morning air. If the ether didn't work, a quick run down the slope to the bottom yard, in-gear, clutch down, edge forward, faster, faster, then Dad would drop the clutch, the tyres would bite on the rough lane and the engine fire up. Dad, his flat cap on backwards so it didn't fly off, turned the tractor on a diff-lock sixpence, looking triumphant from the thrill of the jump-start.

He knew that I knew how to start the Massey-Harris. Choke out, gear stick in neutral and turn the key. I did it once. Scared myself witless. Now the key is gone, and a large screwdriver inserted into a secret, hidden place under the bonnet of the big red machine brings it to life. He knew I wouldn't dare now, such was the fright I gave myself.

I loved a ride on the tractors with him when he let me, clinging on as we bumped over ruts and furrows, bounced around, shaken to the bone. He would let us ride on the trailers, clinging to the hecks, the smell of warm tractor blown back from the engine, into our faces, mixed with the rushing fresh air. Or even better, when I got to lie on top of a full load of straw, pressed flat to the bales, hoping Dad would give the low branches a wide berth and praying the bales had been stacked tight and would not move. On the tarmac lanes, Dad would give the tractor 'the beans' and the wind nearly lifted me up as I pressed myself into the top of the stack as hard as I could.

There was a tall stile at the end of the stack yard. Four flagstone steps up and four down the other side, over the high wall and into Long Donald's garden with its neat rows of green-bean canes supporting only spiral-twisted and tough-as-old-boots beans by now. Next, an out-of-control splurge of rhubarb with huge green leaves and bitter, dark red stalks and Christmas Brussels sprouts in the weedy plot. Long Donald – he *was* quite tall – is Ian's Dad, and Ian is my best mate. But I didn't have time for best mates on work mornings.

I would head further up the slope with the walls high either side of the me, the tractor tracks set deep into the hard-packed lane. I kicked out at loose stones and the sharp ones pressed through the soles of my boots. I paused and our Border collie, Moss, caught up, getting on a bit now, but still with a twinkle in his eye, breathing fast, tongue lolling out of one side of pink and orange flecked chops, his soft black and white under-belly matted with cow muck and straw. I patted his head; he licked my wrist and pressed close to me. I smiled at him and tickled his chin, and he gazed back at me like I was the only one who really paid him any attention at all.

Together, as we passed the orchard entrance, Moss instinctively crouched a little lower, gait slowing, ears flattened to his head, all instinct, detecting movement. The old sows in the orchard were sleepy, tucked into the piles of straw in their corrugated tin arcs, stuffed to bursting with early morning windfalls, gratefully snaffled. The cidery aroma from over-ripe fruit wafted between the scraggy trees. The leaves rattled and rasped in the breeze, alternately green and silver as the wind whipped them around.

71

Out into the top lane, the high enclosing walls of the yard behind me now, the sky opened up, suddenly big. I went straight on, through the gate. I skirted the single-strand electric fence. Out in the fields together, Dad thought it was hilarious to grab this, holding my hand at the same time and seeing the shock go to earth, right through me. I was much older and much wiser now, and far too grown-up to hold hands with my Dad anyway. Into the open fields, Moss scooted ahead after the birds or rabbits he imagined to be behind every clump of nettles.

I crossed the top field and headed to the gate leading to the next one. The wind caught the flaps of my duffel coat and I pulled the hood up to cover my ears. I felt the gap between my shorts and my wellies for the first time. Goosebump knees. My long socks had disappeared into my wellies, but my toes were as warm as toast.

Moss skirted the field, seeing what he could scare up in the wall bottoms, and joined me to be let through the next gate. I opened the gate and closed it carefully behind me. Moss followed, looking interested. The dairy cows grazed quietly, some looked up, not expecting Moss and me.

'Come by,' I said softly, and Moss headed off left in a big half circle, hugging the far wall; in seconds he was at the end of the field and behind the cows. He darted left and right and back again, getting closer. The cows lifted their heads wearily, perplexed, but used to the routine; they started to move towards me. I set off right and looped around to join Moss behind the cows as we moved them gently to the field entrance.

Then the cows stopped. They clustered around the gateway, paddling in the mud that never seemed to dry, right by the stone trough and gate. Confused, they shuffled, uneasily, watching Moss as he watched them, now crouched low. Then the cows stood quiet. Moss looked to me for instruction. One of the cows tried to move away from the others and Moss immediately brought her to heel with a quick dart left and right. They pressed close to the gate, a solid mass of cow.

Dad had always said to make sure to close gates behind me. I had closed the gate. Bringing the cows in for milking was not happening as I had planned. Moss continued to press. I sat down on the damp grass. The cows have nowhere to go. I couldn't get to the gate; there were too many cows in between and they suddenly seemed very big.

Two cows made a break to the left and others followed in all directions, I jumped to my feet and took some steps back; Moss didn't know which way to go first. The herd split and spread. The gate appeared and leaning on it, grinning, was Dad.

'Ey up, what you up to?' asked Dad.

'I was getting the cows in for milking for you,' I replied.

'A bit late son, the cows were milked two hours ago. Come on.'

I climbed halfway up the gate and two big hands lifted me the rest of the way and let go a little bit too far off the ground. My chilly knees buckled a bit when my wellies reach the grass. He did that on purpose. He smiled. Moss scooted under the lower bar of the gate and fell in behind. As we headed back to the lane, my hand slipped into his. 'Let's get some breakfast,' he said.

11

HARVEST

The daily chores of farm work were overlaid by the seasonal rhythms of planting and harvest. While still at Top of the Town Farm, Dad grew thin crops of wheat or barley in the unpromising soil. He was convinced of his own superior ability to grow the very best grass, but his attempts to grow pretty much anything else were usually – literally – quite patchy. But a crop of barley provided both feed and bedding and, ever ready to have a go, seeds would be planted in spring using an old seed drill he had bought for nothing, or when this broke, he would walk the field, seeds in a bag under his arm and scatter them on the ground by hand, just like in the Van Gogh picture, before passing through the field with a light harrow to cover them over.

The abiding memory of harvest time is of long sunny days with warm gentle breezes and a sense of anticipation that I still get today, looking forward to the plenty a good harvest provides as the crops turn golden yellow in the sun. When we

75

were very young, in the early sixties, harvesting was done by threshing teams, going from farm to farm, often moving from south to north following the ripening of the crop, a few weeks of intensive work, towing the threshing machines with them. The threshing gangs were a dying breed as new harvesting methods, far less labour intensive, took over. The early sixties probably saw the last of these and our place must have been one of the last few to employ this way of getting the crops in.

Long before combine harvesters were common around our way, there were various tractor-drawn machines which seemed to spend most of the time broken down. One of these was a binder, a sharp vibrating cutter bar at the front and a windmill-like affair that lined up the barley as it was cut and tied it into neat bundles. Dad would hitch the binder to the tractor and set off down the fields cutting the barley in neat rows, the binder tying the stalks with the ripe heads of grain still attached. The bundles would then be stacked into 'stooks', little tepee shapes, in rows along the field, to dry out in the sun.

If the sun shone and the stooks stayed dry, a trailer would be hitched to the tractor and the freshly cut corn collected in, ready for the arrival of the threshing crew. The team consisted of a bunch of rough-looking men burnished mahogany brown in the summer sun. They brought with them the fearsome bulk of the threshing machine, a heaving clanking monster that was used to separate the barley from the straw.

The threshing machine would be parked in our top field. A long thick drive belt would be connected to the pulley wheel of a large tractor at one end and a huge cast iron flywheel on the threshing machine at the other. The tractor would start and with a grinding of gears, engaging the power to the belt, the thresher would come to life. Dust would fly everywhere as the insides of the machine shuddered into motion, and the straw walkers and riddles used to shake the barley seeds from the straw started to vibrate. The noise of the tractor and the motion of the thresher seemed to shake the ground. Dad told us to stand well away, fearing that the flappy belt driving the whole thing would fly off at any minute and decapitate an innocent bystander.

Once the machine was running to the satisfaction of the threshing crew, sharp knives would cut the string binding the barley. Pitch forks, expertly employed, heaved the stalks into the top of the thresher. The barley would come trickling down a spout on the side of the machine and into large hessian sacks, to be lifted onto a nearby trailer and taken down to the feed store. Straw would spew out of the back end of the machine.

The hot air was thick with dust. Clouds of fine chaff would fly everywhere. The threshing crew would have their shirts off by now and sweat would pour from them as the crop was fed into the jaws of the machine. The thresher was only there for the day and the whole harvest had to be processed before dark. The noise was deafening, the motion constant. The fumes from the tractor powering the threshing machine would radiate out in waves tinged with smoke from the hot oil, the air above the engine, a rippling heat haze.

Occasionally, the team would call a halt. Mum would bring home-made lemonade from the house in big jugs, along with cheese sandwiches, fist-sized chunks of thick cut bread, which were devoured quickly by the hungry workers. Then, of course, there was a huge slab of cake for each man, to be washed down with strong tea.

After the short break, the hectic pace resumed. Tractors and trailers came back and forth from the fields, and another tractor towed away the grain trailer. It was a spectacle that attracted an audience: neighbours came to see what all the noise and frantic activity was all about, and people from the village would stop and stare, not knowing that they were seeing harvest done in this way for the very last time, the threshing machines being consigned to agricultural museums or to the scrap yard not long afterwards.

By the time the work was done, the setting sun would be turned hazy and blood red by the dust. The stacks were topped off with a neat slope to allow the rain to run off and thick green canvas tarpaulins would be lifted over the stacks and weighed down with large stones tied to guy ropes.

Tired men leaned on their pitchforks, scratching and slapping itchy skin. Barley dust and the tiny black harvest bugs got everywhere. Bits of straw stuck in the hair and lodged in every fold. The chaff would lie like snow around machines, now still, the engines still tinkling as they cooled. Buckets would be dipped in the stone trough and water poured over heads and down backs to ease the irritation. Boots would be removed and bits of straw emptied out, socks shaken, hair ruffled, plumes of dust taking to the air. Then the tractor would be decoupled from the flywheel and hitched to the front of the thresher ready to tow it away to the next farm for more of the same the next day. The season for the threshing team was short, but the days were long and hard.

Harvesting the barley might be book-ended by hay time. Sometimes the heavy soils would yield up two crops of lush grass for cutting and making into hay and sometimes the sun would shine just long enough to dry the newly mown grass and allow it to be baled. A wet summer meant little hay of any use because the cut grass needed to be dry to be stored. A successful hay time meant happiness with plenty of feed for the coming winter.

The hay fields would be set aside, the cows or sheep not allowed to graze them. The meadows would have been given an extra helping of manure in the autumn and by late spring would be lush, the grass jewelled with wildflowers, the bottom of the sward rich with clover. It needed to be cut before the grass got too stalky. All the nutrients are in the darker green blades of grass.

The field would be cut and the grass laid in neat rows behind the tractor and the rattling cutter bar of the mower. Young hares would bolt out in front of the tractor, just in time to avoid been mown down. They would zigzag for the nearest safe haven, chased by the dogs, but too tricky to be caught. Silent prayers would be offered for consecutive drying days; the weather forecast was watched with keen interest. The aroma of freshly mown grass filled the air.

If the sun shone, the grass dried quickly and next day Dad would be back in the field with the swath turner, a crane fly of a machine with four revolving wheels with long tines on each, that somehow brought to the surface all the wetter grass and stood up the rows, to let the breeze blow through. We called this machine the woofler. After two more days of repeated turning and drying – assuming the rain didn't come – the hay could be baled. If it rained, more woofling would be needed to shake out the moisture. Rain would make this a losing game as the cut grass quickly turned to mush, which no amount of turning could ever get dry. Even if it could eventually be baled, the bales would be heavy and wet, and would soon mould and rot in the barn.

A dry hay time had all the joys of the corn harvest. The woofler would make its final appearance, this time to put two rows into one bigger one, to make sure the baling could be as efficient as possible. Great elongated piles of grass ran the length of the field and the baler would make short work of compacting the grass into solid bales. Tractors with front loaders would dart about the field, spike the bales and drop them onto trailers where they would be neatly stacked ready for the slow journey back to the stack yard. This was urgent work, driven on by any threat of a change in the weather. It was also dangerous work for small boys and we were kept well out of the way of the machines. It turned out the safest place would be on the footplate of the tractor with Dad, towing the baler. Up high on the tractor, we could look over the field, feel the breeze in our hair, and smell the hot oil from the engine as it strained to pull the baler through the heavy crop. The tractor rocked gently from the motion of the baler it was towing.

Once the hay crop was gathered in, it could rain all it liked. The cows would be let into the hay fields to scour off the margins and glean any last bits of the sweet cut grass. If it rained now and stayed warm, the grass would grow back and another, lighter hay crop might be taken in late summer. After this, a thick coating of well-rotted manure would be spread in anticipation of the next growing season.

Dad would take pride in how much grass he could grow. I am sure it was his plan that the pig unit would provide rich fertiliser for the surrounding fields and that these would then produce the feed for the beef cattle. At Scout Dike and Greetham Lodge, he would harvest the grass for silage: it was piled high at the back of the farm and rolled back and forth with the heaviest tractors to squash the air and moisture out, letting the anaerobic bacteria do their stuff and ferment the grass into high-energy winter feed. The silage 'clamp' would be covered with huge plastic sheets weighted down with old tyres, and left to warm up, the smell of the grass turning gradually to a sweet, fermented odour.

How much feed and bedding we would have for the animals over the winter depended on the richness of the harvest. An abundance would mean better-fed cows, more milk and a bigger milk cheque from the dairy. More feed would mean beef cattle would be ready for market more quickly and another vital pay day. Although it was always at the whim of the weather, the harvest mattered a lot to the economics of the farm. A light harvest meant more expensive bought-in feed, slimmer margins and limited scope to boost milk yields with more and better quality feed. A good harvest must have allowed Dad at least a glimpse of satisfaction.

12

THE FARM SHOP

After we moved to Scout Dike, making a good living from pig farming became very difficult as the recession bit, driven by miners' strikes and culminating in the darkness of the three-day week. Dad had given up his work for the Ministry and the farm was the sole source of income. Driven by necessity, the idea of opening a farm shop started to form. Dad reasoned that with money short, people might want to buy in bulk, directly from the producer, especially now that many owned freezers.

Thinking about and planning this new venture in minute detail, Dad had overlooked a few key points. Firstly, that he would have to deal with members of the public, never his favourite group of people; second, that he would have to employ staff and he might even have to talk to them. Thirdly, apart from killing a pig for our own use about twice a year, he had never done anything like this before, ever, or even anything a little bit like this. He was way out of his comfort zone. Typically, this did not stop him or even slow him down a little.

His idea was to take animals from the farm to the local abattoir, bring the carcasses back and cut them up how the customer wanted, then bag the joints and chops and label them for people to put in their new freezers. Dad began the process of transforming our garage into a butcher's shop.

Dad had no formal training at all in the skills required to cut up a carcass. But with his usual practicality, he learned quickly. If we were ever out in town, he would linger outside butchers' shops, looking at the displays in the windows, learning how the carcasses were cut up to give the optimum return. This was just common sense as far as he was concerned.

As ever, he wanted to do things as efficiently as possible; time was of the essence and cutting chops with a conventional knife and saw would take far too long. So he invested in a huge band-saw which terrified the life out of pretty much everyone but which enabled him to reduce a full loin of pork into two dozen chops in seconds.

He took on George, a retired butcher who lived locally. George was an artist with a butcher's knife, and Dad watched him like a hawk as he skilfully guided his knife around the complicated shoulder bones and sinews of a forequarter of beef, cutting away gristle and fat to reveal beautiful crimson joints. George knew how to extract maximum value from the carcass, minimising waste, something that appealed greatly to Dad, who rapidly learned to do it himself.

The business expanded quickly as more and more people bought freezers and a series of characters came to work in the shop, wrapping and packing the meat that the butchers cut up.

One of the butchers was called Cherry. If he had a first name, we never knew it and it was never used. He was a good butcher but a lousy timekeeper, and a good day for Cherry was turning up on time. He would walk in, trailing a plume of smoke from a recently stubbed-out cigarette, and with a cheeky grin and a pat on the bottom for one of the girls. Most of the time this earned him a slap that would have dissuaded most people, but Cherry was ever hopeful that one of the team might succumb to his charms.

Most weeks it seemed that Cherry would do something so awful that Dad would have to sack him. But he always turned up the next day as if nothing had happened, with the same cheeky grin, and nothing was ever said. Sometimes he stayed sacked for two or three days, no doubt working off a hangover. Dad fretted when he wasn't there, as there were not enough hours in the day to get the growing number of orders out, though he was never bothered enough to call Cherry up and find out where the bloody hell he was. A few days later, he would walk in, unshaven, hair greasy, all toxic breath and a sheepish grin.

'Have you missed me?' he would ask the girls.
    'Oh yes,' they might reply, 'like a bad cold after it's better'
    'Give us a kiss then.'
    'Sod off, Cherry.'

Dad would say nothing, except perhaps a terse 'morning'. Cherry would put on his white coat and apron and get to work.

The shop was hard, physical work. Staff came and went, most unable to adapt to the long days, the standing, the lifting and carrying, and the cold hands from the meat from the large cold stores. But two of 'the girls' stuck it out. One was a burly, scruffy miner's wife, who worked only to earn enough to look after her scraggy horses, of which she smelled. She was strong and willing and worked quickly and quietly, both big pluses in Dad's book. If Cherry offered any of his lip, she had no hesitation in whacking him. The other was a small, fragile, bottle-blonde woman, whose lack of stature belied her strength and stamina. More lippy than the other, she too was a good worker, pausing only in her work to flirt with Cherry, in whose eyes you could see the flicker of hope, clouded with uncertainty. He was never quite sure how to deal with a dose of his own flirty behaviour.

While staff came and went, one in particular stayed a lot longer. This was Dawn, who came with the horsey lady one day and stayed. She was a girl of few words and just got on with her work. Pretty soon, she and John started to notice each other and being about as good at talking as one another, even started to have conversations. The only place John was ever likely to meet a girl was at work, and Dawn fitted right in. They were married eventually although how John managed to propose – all that talking – is a mystery!

At busy times, the shop was truly a family affair. John was more than capable of looking after the farm, and while Dad saw the farm as his domain, his time was increasingly devoted to running the new business. Mum would wrap and pack, sort out payroll, make up the customers' bills and take turns to do deliveries.

I learned to drive by doing deliveries with Mum. I refused to drive if Dad was in the car, such was his constant stream of instructions to either 'stop driving in the gutter' or 'come out of the middle of the road'. Confidence shattered; I couldn't win. As soon as I passed my test, I was pressed into delivering, haring down the country lanes loaded with orders in our new van. On Friday nights, I would head towards Barnsley, where the miners' families were ready customers. Arthur Scargill had made sure that his union members were some of the best-paid workers in the country, so paying for the best steaks and chops was never a problem.

Some of the miners were big men, the smile lines on their faces etched black with coal dust. Others coughed constantly, diminished by the dust on their chests. They would all call me 'love', as all men referred to one another in Barnsley. Big wads of notes were pulled from back pockets for the fillet and sirloin steaks I delivered to their tiny, cramped kitchens. These would be picked up and carefully examined like precious objects by all members of the family.

The miners' houses always seemed to be full of steam from twin-tub washing machines, mingled with cigarette smoke and a sour back note of boiled cabbage. The men would have cigarettes hanging from the corners of their mouths, balancing precariously on their bottom lips. The women would hold their ciggies between two fingers pointing skywards, one elbow resting on an ample hip. They called me 'love' too.

The tiny kitchens would be the gathering places for several generations: the wife's mother or a sister would stand around in the kitchen smoking, chatting and preparing food; kids would dodge in and out; and little ones wrapped themselves around their mothers' legs. Often my delivery would be divided up between several households. These families were always warm, generous and welcoming, pleased with what I delivered and grateful.

One of our regulars was a Mrs Sidebottom. We thought perhaps she was the wife of a pit supervisor or 'management'. She had airs and graces which she clearly thought set her apart, that is above, everyone else. She would call her order in, using her very poshest voice, but when we asked her for her name and address she very carefully enunciated 'Mrs Side-Botham', with a distinct pause after the word 'Side'. Poor Mrs Sidebottom became something of a running joke, one that lasted for many years in our family, the falsely posh always being described as having a touch of the Side-Botham's about them.

Far less posh was Mr Armitage, a lovely old gentleman who lived by himself in a tiny terraced house close by. We would deliver a small package of fresh meat, the same order, every week. Instead of money, he would pay us with things he had found or made. He liked to walk for miles along the little back roads that laced the hill sides, collecting elderflowers or blackberries, crab apples or wild strawberries. He made elderflower cordial, properly fizzy elderflower champagne, blackberry wine and blackcurrant syrup from the fruit from his back garden. He made crab apple jelly and rose hip jam; whatever he could find was made into something useful and we were pleased to 'barter' his produce for ours. He loved to chat, so we made sure he was the last of the deliveries so we could stay a while; he always had something interesting to tell us about what he had found and what he had made.

As the meat business grew, Dad became an avid reader of the weekly magazine *Meat Trades Journal* and determined that in order to make real money out of his butchery business he would have to invest in an industrial mincer and a sausage-making machine. This way he could make minced beef, which he thought would sell well. He could also use up some of the offcuts and less popular parts of the pork pigs, to make added value lines like sausages and burgers.

Making hundreds of pounds of fresh sausages became my Saturday job. We even had our own special recipe, perfected over multiple breakfasts. We used only prime meat, carefully cutting away the fat to make our minced beef as lean as it could be and to make sure our sausages were meaty-pink rather than white and fatty. Dad would experiment with new flavours, adding in sage or tomatoes to see how they sold. But my prime pork sausages were the best sellers, and I must have made tons of them over the years. At Christmas time I couldn't keep up with demand.

Early Saturday, before our regular shop customers started to arrive, I assembled the ingredients, mixing them in large bowls before feeding them into the mouth of a large commercial mincer from which a long stream of pink sausage meat spewed. This was then transferred to the filling machine. This was a cylinder with a piston. The meat was loaded into the top and the lid fastened tight. A lever was pressed with the knee to make sure both hands were free and fresh sausage meat would pour from a spout into skins attached to a nozzle. I would fill the skins and link them to form long, plump, pink, shiny sausages. I was pleased and proud of my dexterity and loved the fact that I had found something that *I* could make. My brothers, all practical and good with their hands, usually made things, not me. But I could now create things people actually wanted to buy in large numbers. It was intoxicating!

I loved the repetitive, rhythmic nature of linking sausages, how it allowed a certain amount of time to dream and plan and scheme. I was truly turning into my father's son. My plotting was mainly about how I would achieve Total World Domination with my special recipe sausages. I devoured the *Meat Trades Journal* too and went to the butchery fair in Harrogate for sausage-making tips. I imagined having my own factory, with all the latest equipment for making the very best sausages in huge numbers. I did some rough costings and multiplied the profits up by the massive volumes I would surely be making. I was going to be a pork-sausage millionaire before I was twenty. A porky plutocrat. My own sausage empire.

An acquaintance of Dad's worked for Associated Dairies, who had a meat factory to supply their Asda stores. Dad wrangled a trip for us around this processing plant, where tons of ingredients were chopped in seconds, the sausage meat then automatically tipped into automated fillers and then through a special twister that turned long sausages into smaller chipolatas. All a very long way from my Saturday-morning dreaming. The fresh sausages flowed out in a relentless stream, as fast as a team of women in floppy blue hairnets could pack them. This was the start of my life-long fascination with food and factories. I could stand and watch production lines for hours. The idea of making things that people wanted to buy stuck with me for life and my 'world-domination' sausage plan was the first of many plans I hatched over the years.

My sausages were certainly in demand with the public, and we started to supply pubs, local shops and work canteens, as well as selling through our own shop. My bangers were developing a reputation and soon we were expanding the range. Dad also bought a machine that pressed my seasoned lean beef into succulent burgers automatically, stocking them in packs of six, ready for sale. Soon, my burgers were popular too. Because they were mainly meat, they didn't shrink like inferior ones. I would experiment with new recipes, testing them on the family.

Soon the shop started to dominate our lives in a way that Dad had never intended. Demand started to far outstrip the ability of the farm to supply. We would be out of the door early, on the way to the meat market for fresh supplies as well as making late deliveries three nights a week. Fifteen- and sixteen-hour days in the shop became normal and there was always the farm to run as well.

The shop brought Dad into closer contact with the public than he could ever have imagined. It was not in his plan to have people calling in orders at all hours of the day and evening, and sometimes over the weekend. But this also threw into his path some enduring characters. Billy was a customer at the shop. He would turn up late on a Friday afternoon, just as we would be loading up the vans for the deliveries that evening. Billy never took the hint that he might be in the way, and he would prop himself up in a corner by the entrance and watch the activity. Every now and then he would stand outside and have a cigarette before resuming his place.

Billy didn't say much, so there were long awkward silences which Dad felt compelled to fill. Unfortunately, this was interpreted by Billy as an invitation to stay and chat, even though we were clearly rushed off our feet trying to get everything done. He seemed content just to hang around. we reached the conclusion that he would rather stand in a draughty doorway or just outside having a fag than go home. To be honest, this was not particularly difficult to understand. At home, his formidable wife was well known to all of us as our teacher at primary school. If she ruled home life with the same ruthlessness as she controlled her class, God help Billy.

Sometimes he would stay for an hour, sometimes more. We never broke stride to speak to him. He might say something, and we might answer; if he was in the way, which was not unusual, we would likely ask him to shift. But somehow Billy became our Friday night fixture, and Dad liked to wind him up at every opportunity.

Billy was a Freemason and over many months, persuaded Dad,

much against his better judgement, to come along to the local lodge. This was pretty much against everything we expected of our father, who as he got older and busier became devoutly unclubbable. He brought to the Masons an irreverence that was more in character. Referring to them only as the 'black-hand gang', he would head out to lodge gatherings in his only and therefore, best suit. I think he was surprised at how many people he knew who were Masons. Many were customers of the shop.

It didn't last long. The pompous rituals and rules quickly turned him off, much to Billy's disappointment. Dad taught us the special secret Masonic handshake and for years afterwards I would try it out on people to see if there was any response. I am not sure I did it right to be fair, which perhaps explains why it was never reciprocated.

The shop started as a necessity and ended up dominating my parents' lives for a while. The money that they made eventually enabled them to buy Greetham Lodge, meaning Dad could get back to the farm.

13

HOLIDAY

The farm held the family captive to its daily chores. The farm shop even more so. Our friends from school were often off to Bridlington, Scarborough, Filey or, for the adventurous ones, Skegness. Our holidays were few and far between and we holidayed as a whole family, only once. When John and I were small, and Dad's farming enterprise was a more manageable size – probably at Mum's insistence – a trip to Butlins in Minehead was booked.

Getting ready to go away, even for a short time, involved planning and instructions and jobs that absolutely could not wait for our return. Dad's brother, who was generally regarded by his younger sibling as 'about as much use as a chocolate fire guard' when it came to farming, would be pressed to action. He would be charged with the simple tasks of feeding round and bedding down while Dad was away. Nothing too complicated of course. If Dad could have trained the farm dogs to bite his brother every time he touched anything he shouldn't, he would have done.

Dad would stride around the place with his brother in tow, issuing detailed instructions in a never-ending stream, telling him to watch out for this animal and to keep an eye on that cow, just in case it started to give birth while we were away – heaven forbid. The brother knew that when he was left in charge, he could never win. Nothing would be done right and all he could hope was that nothing died on his watch. Consequently, his expression varied from exasperation, then boredom, to the resentment of being told how to 'carry on' by his younger brother.

Meanwhile, Mum would be dressing me and John in clean holiday clothes with instructions not to get them dirty before we left. She would be cramming spare clothes into a tattered brown leather case that bore all the marks of being well travelled even though it saw the light of day less than once a year. She would be filling giant Tupperware boxes with provisions, as if shops didn't exist where we were going. Pop bottles would be filled with sweet drinks and a bag of apples placed under the front seat of the car.

Slowly, the car was filled to bursting with wind breaks, beech balls, umbrellas, cases, coats, wellies and food. Good intentions to try and leave on time were long forgotten as Dad anxiously patrolled the farm, checking everything and giving ever more details to his brother. Such was the lack of trust that it seemed that he was asking his brother to do this and that, yet, what he really meant was, for Christ's sake, don't do anything! Just in case you don't do it right.

It is never, ever a good idea to start a long car journey with a row. Hours after the imagined leaving time, Dad would appear at the kitchen door, still in wellies and work clothes. He would dash upstairs pursued by a stream of questions:

'Why do you always do this?'

'What was so important?'

'Why couldn't that job have waited?'

But within minutes, Dad would be down again, scrubbed and fresh, his hair wet and slicked back, bits of bloody toilet roll stuck to where he had nicked his chin in the hurry to shave and look presentable.

We would be chivvied into the jam-packed car, shoe-horned into the back seat alongside cases and carrier bags filled with essentials for the holidays. And then we would be off, until we weren't. At the gate to the farm, the car would come to a screeching halt and Dad would leap out and dash back to issue a last instruction or do a little job he'd forgotten. Mum would quietly seethe. Dad would have the good grace to look a little embarrassed, though never apologetic. He would jump back in and, with tyres spinning and throwing a hail of stones that rattled around the wheel arches, we would be off, Dad driving frantically fast, trying to make up for lost time. Apart from Mum telling him to slow down, silence prevailed for the first part of the journey.

The air of holiday anticipation was soon replaced by that slightly warm, heady, sicky feeling of the early stages of motion sickness. Mum would delve deep into her enormous bag for a little foil strip of tablets called Kwells which were supposed to help, but they tasted so disgusting that just swallowing them down doubled the nausea. Rearranging the carefully crammed back seat so I could shuffle near to the open window, the journey would pass, me with my head out of the car like a mournful spaniel, the rushing air taking the edge off the nausea, with Mum constantly asking if I was all right and Dad telling me that if I was going to be sick, could I aim it out of the car rather than inside. Too often my aim would be off though, and there would be long stops at the side of the road for a change of clothes or to mop the spew from the footwell. Mum would do that thing with her dainty hanky, making it into a point over her finger, dabbing it on her tongue, and jabbing it at any stray dribbles of sick on my face.

Mum had booked three days at Butlin's holiday camp in Minehead. A long drive from our Yorkshire home for just three days. Mum and Dad had decided that it would be best to travel down overnight, to avoid the traffic and to get there in good time next day to enjoy everything that the holiday camp had to offer. The evening was cool and John and I were tired. I suppose they reasoned that if I was asleep, I would not be filling the car with sick. The timing of the departure and the prospect of driving through the night to be there by the next morning heightened the sense of anticipation.

Before motorways, the major A roads between important towns were the way to go. Mum had the *Reader's Digest Book of the Road* open, balanced on her lap navigating through the East Midlands, and down through Birmingham as John and I snoozed. In Bristol, we had a bleary-eyed wake-up as we drew into an all-night petrol station, but we soon were fast asleep again.

Early dawn, we woke up, parked in the opening to a field, the morning sun low in the sky, hazy through the low mist that hovered above the ground, me curled up on the back seat, my little brother fast asleep on the parcel shelf above me, Mum and Dad snoozing quietly in the front. The dawn chorus has never seemed so loud as Dad gently opened the car door, slipping his feet into his shoes and heading off for a pee in the field.

We were all groggy, punch-drunk with tiredness, and as Dad returned, Mum broke out the flask for a cup of lukewarm milky-weak tea. Sandwiches, carefully packed, were retrieved from the boot as John stretched, rolled and landed on top of me in the back seat. Living a farming life makes everyone accustomed to early starts. The tea and sandwiches prepared us for the day ahead and we were on the road again before most of the rest of the traffic.

Mum had booked a 'chalet' at Butlin's. These were built of wood, were not the least bit chalet like and stood in long rows, like the ones we saw in prisoner-of-war films on TV. We had arrived at what Dad immediately called Stalag Luft Minehead. The slightly claustrophobic feel of the place was not helped by the high earth banks surrounding the camp which kept the flood water out in winter (and the people in, in the summer?).

We collected the key to our chalet from the reception area, where the famous Butlin's Redcoats patrolled, greeting guests and playing silly jokes on car-weary travellers. We were filled with excitement. Dad was suspicious of anyone who thought they knew how to make him have a good time.

Butlin's Minehead had only been open for five or six years when we visited at the end of that summer, but the constant churn of visitors through the peak holiday months was taking a toll and the place already seemed to be frayed and frazzled, the people running it included. Forced smiles greeted another group of paying visitors.

The chalet was small and plain, the paint thin and faded from the sun, the wind and the corrosive effects of the fine sand that seemed to be constantly in the air. We had bunk beds. John and I squabbled over who went on top. There was a tiny kitchen with a single electric ring, a kettle and a small fridge. The furniture and fittings all had wipe-clean surfaces and seemed fragile compared to the sturdy dark-wood table and chairs at home. Why come away and stay in a place that is not a nice as home, was Dad's usual complaint, but he kept his counsel.

The food Mum had brought from home was a bit squashed, the sandwiches a jumble of mismatched fillings and stray slices of bread, starting to curl at the edges. These were consumed along with tea and what remained of a cake that had travelled even less well.

Then it was off for an explore. The long rows of chalets were bisected with worn out strips of lawn where people were lounging, perhaps in the lee of brightly coloured wind breaks, taking the sun, kicking balls around, parents shouting at kids, kids shouting at other kids. Trampled flower beds looked dusty and desiccated. Sad, stunted palm trees, leaning away from the prevailing wind, provided shade for the few patches of green grass.

John and I were wide-eyed with wonder. We wanted to try everything there was to try, right now; we couldn't wait. Every corner we turned revealed even more exciting things to do. Dad, perhaps exhausted from the drive, counselled caution, telling us we would have lots of time to do everything, so 'let's have a good look round first'.

The whole place was ringed by a monorail, the cars trundling by overhead. We passed the mini golf where teenage boys were trying to get far too familiar with teenage girls, pretending to help with the girls' putting action by wiggling their groins against the girls' backsides, the boys' arms wrapped around the girls' waists, helping them grip the putter properly, to shrieks of laughter.

The outdoor pool was the biggest I had ever seen, completely surrounded by deck chairs, ten or twenty deep, in long ordered rows, every one seemingly taken by uncomfortable men in thick wool trousers, shirts with long sleeves rolled up and flat caps. And yes, even knotted hankies on the head. Most of them looked like fish out of water. Women in modest bathing suits lounged alongside, occasionally glancing towards the pool to make sure their kids hadn't drowned. Any flesh on show was bright red; ruddy noses accompanied burned foreheads and raw shoulders.

Disturbingly at first, a Redcoat might pop up at any moment, to make sure everyone was having the time of their lives, playing practical jokes with pretend buckets of water or making sure that everyone knew that there would be darts in the main pavilion in half an hour, or ping-pong by the pool. None of this impressed Dad much as we strode with purpose around the camp.

At one end of the pool was a fountain where young girls in bikinis, displayed for the boys, looking unimpressed at the boys macho splashy water fights. Beyond that was a boating lake with canoes and rowing boats, the water surrounding scrubby islands with more flower beds, long past their first flush of colour.

We begged Dad for a go in a rowing boat, but he barely broke stride, as if taking it all in would help him re-establish that safe place in his comfort zone. The boating, mini golf and pretty much everything else would have to wait until later.

We inspected the indoor pool and found out where the restaurant was. A large black steam engine seemed to have been parked at random in front of the main building. There was a queue of eager small boys, all waiting for their turn on the foot plate. The wind blew in from the sea, moving the heat around, and sending small particles of sand to sting legs and irritate eyes. We walked and got our bearings, wondering what we might be allowed to do first.

Butlin's was never going to be Dad's natural habitat. Holidays were what normal people did and the message seemed to be that farmers were not normal people. He desired neither 'time off' nor holidays and didn't enjoy either very much. He looked and acted like he was in a foreign land, understanding nothing of the language or customs. While others ambled, he strode, deciding that there was little for him here, plotting his escape already. He didn't possess holiday clothes – or summer clothes for that matter. When it was warm, he would wear fewer layers, when cold, more. He hated to be 'organised' to do anything he didn't want to do.

So the famous Butlin's Redcoats were never going to be Dad's thing. They were there to make sure everyone had fun. 'Whether they wanted to or not,' Dad grumbled. Like pied pipers they would lead long snakes of whooping and screaming kids through the camp from activity to activity. He was naturally suspicious of any type of enthusiasm, particularly of the forced Butlin's variety. He visibly shrank at the thought of being volunteered for some fun.

Eventually, his resolve crumbled, encouraged by Mum and we were allowed a go on the rowing boats, had a ride on the monorail, splashed in the pool until our feet were white and wrinkled and played crazy golf as the sun slowly set. We had the best time. Dad might even have relaxed a bit.

In the evening, after dinner, there would be a stage show, maybe a magician, some singing, dancing, games and – horror – audience participation. So we sat as far away from the stage as we could. My brother and I were allowed to go forward and sit on the floor right in front of the stage with the other kids, necks bent back, heads craning upwards to see, half hoping that the magician would pick one of us to help pull a rabbit out of a hat, but also, anxiously half hoping that we *wouldn't* be picked.

Breakfast the next morning was in a huge building, with a high ceiling, that bounced the noise of a thousand diners around and made the place seem a mad house. Dad had always had issues hearing anything above a background noise, but none of us could hear each other speak here. Large men with plates stacked up to overflowing made sure they 'filled their boots', extracting maximum value from the ample food. Meanwhile the Redcoats were up and about, marching round, collecting kids in a lengthening line, all accompanied by loud music which everyone was encouraged to stamp their feet and clap their hands in time to.

As if he couldn't wait to get away, Dad suggested a 'nice drive' after breakfast, to get to know the countryside and maybe find a beach. All this was code, for *anywhere without Redcoats*. Full of sausages, beans, eggs and a fried slice, our ears ringing from the breakfast cacophony, we headed back to the chalet to get our swimmies and everything we needed for a day on the beach. We piled into the car with a promise of an ice cream once we had found a nice place to stop and headed out of the gate (under the noses of the armed guards and dodging the search lights and machine-gun nests, joked Dad) and into the countryside.

What Dad really wanted was to see the type of farming they did in north Somerset. He drove quickly, impatient to be somewhere more familiar. But the stone banks topped with thick hedges that lined the roads were impenetrable, hiding the farms and the fields. If we saw a gate opening into a field where sheep or cattle quietly grazed, Dad would slam the brakes on hard. There would be a rapid appraisal of the livestock, maybe an approving word or two. Mum would agree and Dad's right foot would hit the accelerator and off we would go again. He might slow the progress to drive past a farmyard. Was he nosey or just inquisitive? Sometimes he would come to a halt, lost in thought and it was all Mum could do to prevent him from driving into somebody else's farm.

After what seemed to us to be relentless hours of twisty-turny roads, John and I bouncing and sliding about in the back, we might eventually stop and be allowed to get out, that sicky feeling starting to creep up through my abdomen and into my throat, my head thudding. We would find a place, seemingly as far away from the crowds as possible, usually some remote cove with a steep climb, down to a narrow strip of sand, the waves washing gently up the beach.

If we could park for free and as long as there was an ice-cream van, that would do very nicely indeed and we would burst from the car, relieved to have stopped, lungs filling with the type of fresh air you only get at the seaside.

Towels, and the windbreak would be retrieved from the boot and we would quickly set up camp, Mum conjuring up some more sandwiches from the depths of her Tupperware stack, or a few breads rolls scrounged from breakfast and somehow filled with sweaty warm cheese and hot tomatoes from the heat of the car. We would quickly wriggle into our trunks under cover of a bath towel, Dad threatening to pull it away at a critical moment to expose our bright white bottoms to any onlookers.

Then we would sprint full tilt into the sea, knees lifting to our chins at the first shock of the cold water, reversing quickly as the waves got bigger, then running back up the beach as fast as we had run down, our arms clutched to our skinny white chests and teeth starting to chatter already. Dad, flat cap firmly on his head, shirt sleeves rolled up, but now shoeless and with his trousers tucked up below his knees, might venture into the waves, but only up to his ankles. Only once that I can remember did Dad expose his lily-white body to the sun, his tanned face, forearms and the back of his neck dark brown in contrast. Mum, who had been wearing her bathing costume, underneath her clothes all along, would sit and watch John and me splashing in the surf, digging little channels in the sand to let the water reach the massive sandcastle Dad had helped us to construct in record time. No more Redcoats, no organised fun, just a 99 Flake each and peace at last.

14

DAYS OUT WITH DAD

Before my brothers and I came along, Mum worked as a Milk Officer for the Ministry of Agriculture. Fresh out of college, she would have had an uphill task gaining the confidence of the hard-bitten hill farmers, who often had no more than half a dozen cows, and still milked by hand or with ancient milking machines. She lived in 'digs' in Huddersfield and travelled from farm to farm, getting to know her patch and the characters on it.

She met my father when he came to an evening meeting she had organised for local farmers in the upstairs room of the Rose and Crown. The irony of their first meeting in a public house was considerable. Dad's father was a heavy drinker and that had put him off drinking for life. And I am sure my maternal grandmother would have thought pubs 'common' and disapproved deeply. She never got over the fact that her eldest daughter met her husband-to-be in a pub, and this contributed to Dad's feeling that he was always looked down on by his mother-in-law. She had high hopes of a good marriage to the son of some prosperous farmer, and these were quickly dashed when her daughter and Dad fell for each other. I am certain that neither of them ever visited the Rose and Crown again; their strait-laced Victorian attitude to pubs as places from which no good ever came stayed with them for life.

While he was building towards having a farm that would, as he put it 'keep him in the style to which he would like to become accustomed', Dad kept up his full-time job with the Ministry of Agriculture. He covered a huge area of North, West and South Yorkshire, inspecting cattle and authorising government subsidy for animals that were of the required quality. In the holidays, I would sometimes join Dad on his visits.

Once he'd finished the morning's jobs around the farm, he would turn to the long list of farmers who had applied to have their cattle inspected. He would plan his journey, mostly in his head, but sometimes with a dog-eared road atlas. This was long before sat-nav and mobile phones and he relied on familiarity, a good sense of direction and if really, really stuck, he might ask someone the way.

Always in a huge hurry and with a sense of urgency that only he seemed to feel, he drove like a mad man, along narrow, twisting lanes up into the Pennine hills. He thought he was Paddy Hopkirk or some Scandinavian rally driver he had seen on TV. He dived into sharp bends, sitting back in his seat, his arms straight on the wheel, accelerating hard along the next straight, tyres squealing round corners and the sides of the car

brushing the grass and low bushes along the sides of the road..
The drystone walls lining the roads looked far too close from
the passenger seat, looming high and immovable through the
window as we skimmed by.

In summer, the car was hot, the leatherette seats sticky, the
feeble blowers on the dash only recycling hot air. The seats
burned the backs of your legs if the car was stood in the sun
for long. With the windows wound down and my face in the
fresh air, the Yorkshire countryside rushed by in a blur. As the
car veered into another corner, I would slide around on the
bench seats, holding tight as he braked for the next bend to
make sure I didn't end up in the footwell. We rumbled over
cattle grids and bucked over hump-backed bridges. A dip in
the road gave Dad the excuse to accelerate and we would giggle
as our stomachs hit our boots. We called it a 'funny feeling'
road. A hump-backed bridge gave him the chance to test the
suspension. He imagined all four wheels off the ground as the
big car lurched over the bumps.

The minor roads were sometimes gated to keep the livestock
that grazed the moors from wandering too far. My job was
to leap out, open the gates, wait until the car was through
and then close them behind and run to get back in, as Dad's
impatient left foot hovered on the clutch. Before I pulled my
door shut, we were off, gravel and stones flying everywhere.
Sometimes he would make to leave me behind, and I would
run until he screeched to a halt, only to drive off as soon as I
caught up. It was like trying to catch a wind-blown paper bag.
Dad thought it was hilarious. I was never altogether certain
he would not absent-mindedly, drive off without me.

As we climbed the narrow lanes into the hills, we passed the many concrete platforms either side of the road where ammunition was stacked out of the way of the German bombs that fell on war-time Sheffield. Soon the green fields, emerald under watery sunshine, gave way to open moorland with purple heather, sometimes with blackened strips where gamekeepers had burned the cover to generate fresh new green shoots for the grouse to feed on.

The hillsides were dotted with scraggy sheep. They grazed either side of the road, their summer fleeces waiting to be clipped, dragging on the ground and hanging in clumps to their skinny carcasses. The ewes were probably looking their worst by early summer, having just had their lambs weaned. Since spring lambing time, the ewes would have suckled one or two hungry lambs, and it showed in their loss of condition. As summer came, some might have been clipped already; the recently shorn always looked alarmed, chilly, and comical.

Little huddles of ewes and lambs wandered across the road, surprised and almost offended to see the approaching car. The lambs would take fright, but the ewes would stand, stupidly defiant in the road, trying to stare us down before realising that the big green car was not about to stop. The grazing was poor and the ground soft and wet. Clumps of rushes grew in acidic bogs. The wind rarely stopped blowing and the weather could turn at any time, sending ewes and lambs skittering to seek shelter. The drystone walls were more broken down and neglected the higher up the valleys we climbed. Some lucky animals had a field barn, low and sturdy, thick walled, with no doors or windows, but shelter all the same. Dad insisted sheep were so daft they didn't know to come in from the cold.

Eventually, we would sweep off the road and onto a rough, unmade farm track, winding uphill to a cluster of remote, dark buildings. Getting closer, large dogs would emerge from rough kennels, often no more than big oil drums laid on their sides with bits of filthy old mattress for the dogs to lie on. They dragged heavy chains tied to frayed collars. They would erupt with fury and run at the car, only to be snapped back when the chain ran out, inches away from the spinning wheels. Smaller, more timid, yappy little dogs came to see what the fuss was about, followed by the farmers, cursing the noise and swinging badly aimed kicks.

The farmers were a rough lot. Dad called these high hills 'cow-boy country'. They wore threadbare tweed jackets, patched and frayed, buttons long gone, wrapped around them tight with string and encrusted with muck. Their flat caps, the peaks shiny-dirty from mucky hands, or home-knit wool hats, were pulled down over hairy ears. Whiskers jutted from determined chins. A Woodbine or a thin roll-up would be stuck in the corner of the mouth. Wellies were black and turned down at the tops to reduce the rub of wearing them all day. Trousers flapped in the breeze, hands buried deep in pockets, shoulders hunched. Gruff greetings were exchanged. Wives would appear to see the visitors, wrapped tight in full-length aprons, arms folded against the wind, and sometimes a few scruffy kids would be playing in the dirt with the dogs or peering round from behind their mothers' legs.

The farmyards were draughty places where doors hung from

single rusty hinges, gates were held up with string and there was an ever-present stench of urine from the cowsheds. Bits of thin plastic shredded by the wind fluttered from stubby thorn bushes. Discarded farm implements were scattered randomly around the farm, left where they had broken down. Decrepit tractors were parked on slopes that they could be run down to jump start. Old cars, with weeds growing through holes in the floors, were left to rot. It was as if the weather was getting the better of everything that once moved, wetting it, corroding it and baking it in the sun in cycles designed eventually to reduce everything to dust.

Always needing to be back for evening feeding at our own farm, Dad operated to a tight schedule. As we rumbled to a halt in the next remote farmyard, he was immediately all business. A thick rubber apron was fetched from the boot and wellies slid onto his feet. The farmers, who, having not seen another person outside family for days – sometimes weeks – wanted to chat. They needed news, gossip, company, relief. But Dad was a moving target now, as if not standing still meant he could not be cornered into a conversation. Social skills were not Dad's strong point, and small talk was not on his agenda at all. He wanted to know where the cattle that he was here to inspect were housed.

The animals would be penned in the corner of a yard or in a dark stone barn. I would stand on a rail and watch Dad expertly sort the cattle. The ones that made the grade would have a hole punched in their ears about half an inch wide so that it was clear that subsidy had been claimed on this animal and could not be claimed again. The rapid click-clack of the hole puncher left a permanent hole and must have been very painful. Dad's forearms and rubber apron would soon be spattered in blood.

Most of these hill cattle were what Dad called 'poor do-ers'. The farmers had penned them in dark barns to hide their lack of condition from the subsidy man. They had large, glassy eyes, set in big heads on skinny necks, sticky out ribs and spines, and their rough, dull hides were stretched thin over their pelvic bones. Their horns were bent at all angles, but sharp enough to give a painful dig in the ribs. They looked cold, even in the summer, and their muscles twitched and shivered as Dad moved them around. They had nothing to cover their bones against the weather on the hills, baked-on mud caked their shins, and shit stuck to their back ends.

The cattle were cross breeds. Dad had no time for the lazy farmers who didn't tend their land and animals. More often than not, these poor hill cattle would need to be brought down to the lower pastures of the narrow valleys to make the grade. The rough, hard-as-nails hill farmers, keen for a government pay-out to keep their farms viable, often disagreed with Dad's low opinion on their poor specimens and would let him know as much. I would be sent to the car in case I learned some new words in the discussion.

When finished, Dad would request a bucket of water to wash his boots, apron and arms. He would disinfect his boots and fill in the forms before giving a copy to the farmer. With few additional words, a revving engine and a hail of loose pebbles, we would be off again, the farm dogs barking at us and running down the lanes, making sure to see us off, a small huddle of farming family looking after us. If it had been human engagement they were after, they were left disappointed.

Mum would have made us some sandwiches, usually a thin slice of ham or some cheese stuck between two slices of plain, white, 'plastic' bread. By now the white-sliced would be squashed flat and warm. Maybe a piece of Mum's cake or a pork pie from a shop on the way would be washed down with weak, and now quite hot, Robinson's orange barley out of a big glass pop bottle. Or if we were lucky, Ben Shaw's ice cream soda, with dandelion and burdock for Dad. We didn't mind warm fizzy pop drunk straight from the bottle. Dad would tap the brakes as I took a swig and the bubbles would shoot up my nose.

Dad would drive like a loon all day. Long before fixed speed cameras, the police used radar guns. One officer would point the gun and record the speed, and radio ahead to a colleague a little way down the road to pull the guilty speeder over. On one of our drives, Dad spotted the radar gun too late. He knew he would be nicked. Thinking quickly, he slammed the brakes on hard and pulled over beside a 'For Sale' sign outside a house. He quickly jumped out and started to inspect the house with exaggerated interest, leaving me in the car wondering what was going on. To their credit, the police officers were having a good laugh, seeing exactly what Dad was up to. He got away with it, of course. He drove fast all his life and never picked up a speeding ticket.

At this time, parts of the district Dad covered were being

carved apart by the new trans-Pennine Motorway, the M62, as it was driven through the deep valleys and over the high hills of the West Yorkshire Pennines above Halifax and Huddersfield. Millions of tons of earth and rock needed to be blasted and moved so the road could be as level as possible. We would park near Rishworth and watch the giant bulldozers and scrapers plough their way through the valley below. Dad knew all small boys loved dumper trucks, and the sheer scale of this was beyond anything we had ever seen.

The high, bleak, windswept land outside Rishworth gave a view of the huge construction site that is now the Scammonden Dam. The motorway runs over the dam wall, bisecting the Deanhead Valley. Everything was on a massive scale; the huge yellow machines crawled slowly over the ground, bending the landscape to their will.

When he was a boy, Dad had seen the building of the Lady-bower and Derwent Dams in Derbyshire, the construction of which had drowned the village of Derwent. Here was where the Dambusters squadron practised their bombing runs in preparation for the raid on the dams on the Ruhr in Germany and Lancaster bombers would have roared up towards the Derwent Dam at the head of the valley, practising their bombing runs, skimming just above the water before climbing steeply, over the dam walls.

Dad would tell of helping to deliver milk to Derwent village before it was submerged beneath the still waters of the reservoir. He must have been around nine or ten at the time, and I imagine him leaving bottles by (now ruined) front doors, walking up garden paths and going from house to house up the steep cobbled street, perhaps getting gruff good mornings from villagers on their way to work or just arriving home from a night shift. The demand for clean water for the growing city of Sheffield, just over the hill, meant that whole communities were uprooted, forcing them to leave houses that had been in their families for as long as anyone could remember. Farmers who had tended the fields on the valley sides had to move animals hefted to these hills for generations as the water slowly rose.

Everything was consumed by the rising water, and when the dam was finished, it took two years for Derwent village to disappear completely. The church steeple was still sticking out when the waters reached the top of the dam. They blew it up in 1947. The hot summer of 2018 dropped the water levels behind the dam so low that the ruined church and a few outlines of drowned houses reappeared for a few weeks. But he was gone too, by then.

15

GRANDAD'S FARM

Don't forget to say 'thank you for having me' before you leave. These were always Mum's last words before we arrived at whichever friends or relations we were about to visit. From then on, we were to be on our best behaviour. Always 'please' and 'thank you'. Never 'Can you pass the bread and butter please?', rather, 'May you pass the Bread and butter please?' We were never allowed to leave the table until everyone had finished, and definitely not without saying 'Please may I leave the table?' And never, ever say 'what?' Always say 'pardon'. These instructions were accompanied by further orders to stand up straight, put our shoulders back and not to mumble.

Visits to Granny and Grandad's farm were a particular trial of Mum's parenting skills. None of us really looked forward to visits to Mum's parents and the 'rules' drummed into us on the way there meant a sense of nervous anticipation bordering on anxiety as we arrived. They lived in a large Victorian house, my abiding memory of which is that the only room that offered any comforting warmth was the kitchen, which smelled of paraffin from the ancient Aga.

We would be scrubbed and changed into best clothes, Dad included. Our hair would be stuck down with water and neatly combed, Dad's with a fresh dab of Brylcream. As soon as Dad had finished his morning jobs, we would be bundled into the car. We would always be late and consequently the journey consisted of Dad driving like a lunatic and Mum asking him to slow down. My parents would bicker good naturedly, usually about why Dad had to come at all.

After an hour and a bit, we would arrive. Granny would be making lunch. It was immediately clear that she had absolutely no idea how much small boys can eat. Luckily, Mum had brought some extra food from home to bulk up our meal. The prevailing mood was one of chilly, awkward silences, as we stood in the kitchen while the grown-ups exchanged polite enquiries and news. Dad looked like he would rather be pretty much anywhere else.

But then Grandad would arrive, trailing his two loyal Jack Russell terriers in his wake.. He would always be pleased to see us, and his warmth immediately filled the room. Playing with the dogs – always excited in the presence of us children – made us all relax a little and provided a welcome distraction.

Grandad's day was dictated by his farming life too, and until he arrived, Dad would be invisible, as if his perception of his mothers-in-law's disapproval of him kept him pinned to the spot, silenced. If my brothers or I spoke, assuming we were asked to speak at all, there would be no 'thee's and 'tha's like we were used to at school, only our very best speaking voices. We too would sit frozen in place by imaginary stern glances. If we escaped the kitchen for the nearby living room with its uncomfortably hard sofa, course upholstery and lumpy cushions, we had to say nowt, and sit up straight, our legs fidgeting, feet itching to be off, faces warm with awkwardness.

But Grandad was always ready with a quick ruffle of our neatly brushed hair and enquiries about our farm at home. His arrival broke the ice and soothed the mood. At last, he had someone to talk to about his favourite – only – subject, his cows. And now Dad had someone to talk to as well. Grandad's conversation picked up seamlessly where he had left off the last time with news about his cows, familiar territory for Dad, who would listen and nod and make agreeing noises and sometimes even exclaim in the right places. Dad would be Grandad's captive audience for the rest of the day, still pinned to the spot, but this time by a continuous stream of news about Grandad's beloved pedigree British Friesians.

Granny was as tightly wound as the clock above the fireplace. We were certain she could drop us where we stood with just a hard stare. She thought children should be seen and definitely not heard. Everything was orderly and still, as if frozen in time, and without Grandad to lighten the day, the silence could be deafening. The big clock in the hall would cause us to jump every time it chimed, and time passed very slowly. She must have dreaded our full-on family visits with the potential for disorder and untidiness we brought. As she prepared impossibly small amounts of vegetables and potatoes to go with the Sunday roast, we would look for opportunities to escape.

By lunch time, we would be feeling like we had not eaten for days. Carving the roast, Grandad would happily chat away to everyone in general and no one in particular, always, still, about cows. Mum and Dad would sit and nod patiently. Grandad might run through the ancestry of a calf born that morning. He would know by heart the sire's bloodline and the dam's closest relatives. Oblivious to the rapidly cooling meat and hungry faces, he would pause regularly, put down the knife as he sought to recall how much milk the mother of the calf had given at her last lactation. Granny knew not to bring the vegetables out until he was well into the carving otherwise they would all go cold.

Eventually, we would eat. Mum's extra food made sure there was more than plenty to go around now. As well as generous slices of rare roast beef and dark brown gravy made in the roasting pan, there would be new potatoes from the kitchen garden, slathered in butter. We would have been sent out to pick some green beans from the garden, too. But Grandad never really paused for breath as on he went detailing the complex bloodlines of his best animals. He was of course the last to finish. We watched each mouthful, urging Grandad not to put down his knife and fork.

Granny, at the other end of the table, doubled the agony. Severe, steady eyes fixed in the middle distance, arms tightly folded, just waiting for an elbow to stray onto the table or for one of us to pick up the wrong knife or hold a fork in the wrong way. We were sure she watched our every move, anticipating some catastrophic breakdown in manners that would confirm what a rotten job Mum was doing bringing us up, no doubt levelling all the blame for this on my father's humble upbringing. We would not dare move until Grandad was done, and we would never depart without elaborate thanks and a chorus of 'Please may I leave the table?' uttered at speed as bottoms slid from chairs.

After lunch we would be allowed out and the grown-ups would move to the best sitting room. This large room was heated by a two-bar electric fire where the open fireplace had been. Even colder than the rest of the house and seemingly only used on Sundays, the cold prevented any smells from the little piles of dried dog poo behind the sofa which we delighted in knowing about, as it was obvious Granny didn't. For Grandad, his little Jack Russell's could do no wrong.

We would escape for a while, knowing that later, when Granny deemed the time suitable, we would be ushered into their formal front room, to sit and listen and fidget and yawn until the relief of home-time, when we could finally leave, exhausted from sitting up straight for so long.

But between lunch and the best-room audience with Granny, we would go and explore. The house and the farm were filled with wonder. Granny had a heart condition and could not manage the stairs, so a lift had been installed in the back kitchen. We would ride up and down just for the novelty of it. We would race the lift up the stairs and down again to see who got there first. Granny would purse her lips like a bulldog chewing on a wasp and fold her arms trying to ward off the din we made.

We would be shooed out into the fresh air where there was the outside loo, almost covered in honeysuckle in summer, always three degrees colder, and there was always a good selection of very large spiders. There were stacks of straw to be clambered over and an essential visit to Grandad's specially built bull pens, where the unimaginably huge animals moved slowly around, beady eyed, breathing heavily, with large brass rings in their noses.

John and I were told that bulls were dangerous and unpredictable. We approached quietly, not wanting to disturb, just in case they bolted clean through the concrete block walls and gored us to death! We crept round the side, just to catch a glimpse through a crack in the door. Peering round the corner, we would see a massive head and a malevolent eye as the bull pressed against the door to see who was looking in. Always startled, we would jump back and skitter back around the corner. Sometimes the massive creature would carelessly swing his huge head, crashing blunted horns on the metal door frame and letting out low, rumbling, guttural, bellows. We would run for our lives, certain the bull was about to break down the steel-reinforced door. If we were feeling really brave, there was a high walkway between the pens which meant a climb up a narrow metal ladder. We could look down into the animals enclosures either side, nervous that they might rear up and grab us by the ankles.

In the hands of my Grandad, the bulls seemed to pose no threat at all. He was only a slight man, but he knew the bulls better than anyone as he had raised them from new-born calves. These animals were the centre of his pedigree Friesian herd, all bred at home. He could trace their bloodlines back over several generations. They were his pride and joy and he would relish leading one of them out by a special pole he attached to the nose ring, so we could get a better look. Even when he was quite frail, he would lead these huge beasts as if they were little kittens. We retreated to the top of the ladder and stayed there.

Grandad loved to show us round his cows. We would collect milk from the dairy and feed the calves while he told us which of his herd was related to this, that or the other. The cows didn't have numbered ear tags; he could identify them just by the markings and he knew the parents, and often their parents' parents and beyond.

He had a little sketch book with two cows in silhouette and he would draw the markings of each one onto these profiles along with any particular markings on the head. The pictures would be faithfully recorded in his Herd Book, the complete record of every animal he had ever owned. Each animal would have a name, part official, part descriptive. A calf with a small splash of black on an otherwise white face would be christened Star, a nose length patch of white on black might mean the calf would be called Blaze. These names would be registered with the British Friesian Society. He knew every single one by its Herd Book name, and of an evening he would pour over this record endlessly, falling silent, lost in thought.

The farm had a modern milking parlour, not at all like the one we had at home. The cows were milked three at a time on a high step, their udders at the dairyman's eye level. A compressor would give a low, monotonous hum. The suction it generated would suck the milk gently from the cleaned udders and squirt it into big glass jars with measuring scales on the sides. The quantity of milk would be recorded for each cow before more compressed air was used to pump the milk to the big, refrigerated milk tank where it would be chilled for collection the next morning.

We would lift the lid of the tank to see the milk being swirled around, dipping Grandad's long-handled sampling cup in for a swig of the coldest, freshest milk you've ever tasted. In the parlour, the gentle *pshhhhht – click* of the milking machines gave an air of calm, although the milker, standing low, at udder level, would always be vulnerable to a large cow emptying its bladder, or worse, onto his head. You had to pay attention or risk a warm shower. The stainless steel, modern parlour was years ahead of what we had at Top of the Town. Every morning a big road tanker would draw into the yard and suck the chilled milk away. We were still putting it in churns at home, lining them up for collection at the side of the road.

After Granny died, Grandad seemed to relax even more, and John and I would be invited to the farm for a few days, usually during harvest time. We would ride high on stacks of bales, helping where we could and cadging rides on tractors. This was until, helping to stack straw bales at the top of a Dutch barn and trying to get out of the way as one of Grandad's workers moved a bale of straw in my direction, I turned around and ran head first into an iron roof strut and cut my head open. A lot of blood, a trip to hospital and some stitches meant that Grandad decided having growing boys to stay might be too much trouble.

Dad rarely came to see his in-laws and he always had our farm to provide ample excuses for staying away. But when he did visit, I am sure he was taking mental notes, gathering ideas he might try at home.

One time, when Mum did manage to take him away from his farm work, he amazed us all. Granny had a piano. It was in the office at the back of the house. If Granny was in the kitchen, we would sneak in and have a look, carefully lifting the lid of the upright, highly polished instrument. Neither Granny nor Grandad played, and I am pretty sure Mum and her sister didn't either. But we would sit and try to tap out 'Three Blind Mice' or 'Chopsticks', making an awful jarring din. Dad came to see what the noise was about. Probably to escape the kitchen conversation. He budged us off the stool and sat down with an elaborate stretching of his fingers, throwing back imaginary tails from his imaginary tailcoat. Then carefully at first, and then faster, he started to tap out a tune. It took him a while, but the melody was there. Once he had it, he repeated it again and again. We were astonished. We crowded round, begging him to play something else. He did! He had never been taught to play, but somehow he magicked a tune from nowhere.

When it was home-time. Mum collected our belongings, washed our cow muck-encrusted wellies and legs under the cold water tap outside and herded us towards the car for the sleepy drive home. But not before we respectfully stood to say 'thank you for having me' to Granny, who stood straight backed, chin pulled back, hands clasped tight in front, forming a handy barrier against any hugging nonsense, stern to the last. No goodbye kiss, no sweets from warm apron pockets, no 'come again soon', and no pleasure taken in her growing grandsons.

16

TRIPS

Trips out always had to be fitted in and were always undertaken at high speed. A trip to the local swimming baths, for example, could be turned into a frantic farce by Dad's over-riding need to save time. He insisted that we changed into our swimming trunks before leaving the house. Clutching rolled-up towels, we would jump into the car and Dad would accelerate hard out of the drive. Passing through villages, dog walkers would do a double take at the car full of nudists. Because, of course, Dad also wanted to save time and had also changed into his fetching pair of olive-green swimming trunks, his outfit set off by a pair of red leatherette carpet slippers.

Arriving at the pool, car doors would swing open and we would run full speed across the car park, clutching sweaty coins in our hands, and hot with squirming embarrassment, one of us would mutter 'three children and one adult for swimming please' to the astonished receptionist. Pausing only long enough to deposit the towels – and Dad's slippers – on the side of the pool, we would leap headlong in, not having broken stride at any stage. Dad would throw himself in, causing a huge splash, and proceed to tip us upside down, lift us high in the air, sometimes pulling at our trunks to show all the other swimmers our skinny arses and generally make a show of himself – and us.

A frantic twenty minutes of splashing and swimming later, Dad would climb out, briefly towel himself down, shout at the rest of us to get out of the pool, now, and before we even had time to complain that we had only just arrived, he would be heading for the door. Dad stormed across the car park again – still in his trunks and slippers, but this time with a towel around his middle, pursued headlong by gang of semi-naked boys, ready to pile back into the car for a breakneck drive home. On warm days, the windows would be wound down so that by the time we got home, we were dry.

Dad's duty of 'spending some quality time with the kids' duly fulfilled, he would be back in his work clothes and wellies almost immediately on arriving home, getting on with his jobs, the whole swimming exercise taking not much longer than an hour, door to door.

We were always taught to eat pretty much everything that was placed in front of us. Both Mum and Dad loved Chinese food and now and then we would head off to Huddersfield or Sheffield for a meal out together. This was usually on a Sunday evening when Dad thought that the restaurants would be quiet and we always went early to make doubly sure that we would be the only ones in at that time. This meant that the service would be quicker, of course.

To speed things up further, Dad would order the set menu. But it would not be too long before he would be huffing and puffing that the service was slow, pointing out the number of waiters who seemed to be doing nothing and wondering what was taking so long. One of the places we went to had a TV, and if there was anything exciting on the screen the service would grind to a halt as the skinny Chinese waiters jabbered to each other. Piles of food, once set on the table, would be wolfed down at speed.

Because neither of my parents touched alcohol at all, a trip to a pub was rare, but when it happened, we went to a large steakhouse on the way to Huddersfield called the Three Owls. One evening, with the whole family present, the rather too posh waiter was taking our order when he asked my little brother how he wanted his steak. Unaccustomed to eating out, my brother thought momentarily, frowned, looked around the table for support, which was not forthcoming, and then said, 'I want it frying please'.

Trips were a treat, infrequent and enjoyed all the more for their rarity. They were enjoyed at full speed because Dad always needed to be back home for urgent farming jobs.

It occurs to me now, that compared to most of my friends, our father involved himself in our lives in ways that other people dads never did. Most of all, we also involved ourselves in his life too: from an early age we worked together, and he paid us for the work we did. He taught us that the best – the only –

way to get to what we wanted was to work for it, to earn the money to pay for it. Be patient, good things will come, but only if you work at it. At work and play we probably spent more time around our dad than most children, for which, with hindsight, we should be eternally grateful.

17

THE GREAT YORKSHIRE SHOW

In the summer we always looked forward to days out at local agricultural shows. The biggest and a must-visit was the Great Yorkshire Show, which took place every year at the permanent show ground just south of Harrogate. This was Mum and Dad's kind of day out and we would start crazy early to get all the jobs done. Oddly, if it was a trip Dad particularly wanted to go on, it was quite possible to get everything that needed to be done completed for an early departure.

But no matter how early we were able to leave, every year we would join the long queue of traffic snaking away from the northbound A1, and through the town of Wetherby. All roads led to Harrogate at show time, and progress would be glacial. He would blame his own laziness for not getting out of bed earlier so that we could have missed the traffic.

The Great Yorkshire was a once-a-year opportunity for the whole farming community to meet up with friends and neighbours. Everyone was in their Sunday best, enhancing the sense of occasion. Market boots would be highly polished, trousers pressed and ties neatly knotted. The show ground was an orderly hum of farming people meeting others they may not have seen for months and swapping stories – but rarely the perpetual complaints for which farmers are well known, The show was a kaleidoscope of activity and it was always difficult to decide where to look first. The natural magnet for small boys was, of course, the huge shiny new combine harvesters. The makers were showing their latest models and groups of children were always keen to clamber over them at the very first opportunity. Scaling the steps to the driver's seat of a huge red combine, sitting at the controls, often barely able to reach the steering wheel, we would look down. but instead of the sea of people below us, we would imagine piloting this huge machine through fields of wheat that stretched as far as the eye could see, like the pictures we had seen of ten combines working in a line, harvesting in the American Midwest, several worlds away from our Pennine home. The tractors were another big draw. These were not like the mud-spattered, second-hand rust buckets that Dad was able to afford for our farm, but huge machines with bright glossy paint and shiny tyres and complicated controls. We would take turns to sit in the drivers' seats, holding the steering wheel and jerking the gearbox up through the ratios. We would press buttons and flick switches, all to no avail as the machines, – thankfully – were dormant, all power disconnected.

Dad wanted to see the livestock show, and he would run his critical eye up and down the long lines of horses, cattle, sheep and pigs being prepared for the ring. There would be rows of cages with fancy bantams and rabbits waiting for the judges. Farmers would bring their best livestock to be judged. Success meant an improved reputation, and maybe better prices for any breeding stock the owners might want to sell. They would go to great lengths to show their animals at their very best, shampooing and combing glossy hides and fluffing up tails. Horses' manes would be plaited and interwoven with bright red ribbons. Hooves and horns would be lacquered and polished, skins burnished with all types of brushes and combs, and special lotions would be added for extra shine.

The owners waited to show their stock in the main ring. Halters would be attached to sheep and cattle and ropes clipped to the nose rings of the huge pedigree bulls. The pigs would be walked out, directed only by a small stick and a thin white plywood board to provide direction. The animals were sometimes reluctant to make their way to the show arena for the parade in front of the judges in an orderly fashion. We secretly hoped that at least one might take exception to all this attention and give its owner a hard time or even make a break for freedom. The owners, serious in their white coats, boots polished to match their animals' hooves, would bring their animals in line and the bowler-hatted judges would walk the lines and inspect the animals before deciding who got the rosettes and certificates. Grandad had dozens of these from his local shows in Nottinghamshire; they were all pinned up in his farm office, and he could still tell you exactly which animal had won what.

Dad wanted to do a bit of business and he would soon be in deep discussions with owners and breeders of pedigree pigs. Maybe he would arrange a visit to see the animals on the owners' farms. He was keen to improve the quality of his stock by introducing new bloodlines, searching for animals that would better convert food to lean meat.

The banter in the cattle sheds was good-natured, many of the farmers knowing Dad from his time with the Ministry of Agriculture. By this time, Mum had decamped to visit the Flower Show and the Women's Institute tents, where there was every type of produce on show, with more rosettes on offer for the biggest or the best. If we drew the short straw, we would have to go with Mum. The family would come together for a quick lunch from a fish and chip van, eating hot salty fries, sitting on the grass in the sun, watching the world go by, fingers and chins getting greasy.

We would pause at the showjumping ring where some of the very best competitors would be put through their paces by riders like David Broome or Harvey Smith, who we had seen on the telly. Or we would watch the hilarity of the pony club gymkhana, chubby children bouncing up and down on little fat ponies just like in Norman Thelwell's cartoons, displaying huge amounts of skill and courage as they negotiated the obstacle courses, or collected objects from the ground without slowing from a gallop.

By mid-afternoon, everyone would be hot and bothered, with aching feet from the constant motion and the desire to see everything there was to see. Our whole bodies craved a sit down, and it would be with great relief that we would slump into the car for the journey home. During the day we would have collected leaflets and brochures from the machinery stands, hoping that one day these wonderful, shiny, complicated bits of kit would grace our farm. In our tired state, all we could do was stare at the pictures and dream.

18

TIMES TABLES

Every morning for five years, we would chant our times tables. Every morning, always starting with 'two twos are four', all the way to twelve twelves. Ever since, I have known my tables by heart, forwards and backwards.

I know the tricky ones like seven eights, or even seven nines, without thinking. I cannot thank our headmistress, Miss Hinchcliffe, enough. My times tables accompany me to work every day. Sometimes if I chant the numbers in my head, the cadence and rhythm take my mind back to school.

Hoylandswaine Juniors and Infants was my first school. It was a typical village school with one large Victorian hall with classrooms leading off and two newer, sixties classrooms for the older children.

There were three teachers. Miss Jackson, who taught infants, was gentle and soft and patient. In her class, we would get a story, first thing, sitting on the floor, clustered around her feet, hanging on every word as she told us about the hare and the tortoise or Tom Kitten. She would read upside down, so we could see the pictures. Then we'd do a bit of writing or a few sums, and maybe some painting or playing with clay. After playtime, it was elevenses. The milk monitor, usually the tallest and strongest boy from Miss Hinchcliffe's class, would deliver the milk to each of the classrooms in one-third-pint glass bottles with foil lids, milk being dished out free in those days, to make sure we all grew up big and strong. The milk monitor position was a prestigious one, given only to the most trustworthy children. I was made milk monitor in my last year at Hoylandswaine, based more on my strength than my reliability.

Mrs Russel, who taught the slightly older kids, was far more demanding than Miss Jackson. We were all scared of her, and she could silence a whole class with a sideways glance. Her classes were good preparation for Miss Hinchcliffe, who was sterner still: an austere, old-school headmistress, tall and imposing, always in tweed skirts and sensible shoes, she would peer at us over half glasses which would be suspended on a gold chain around her neck when not in use. She taught the oldest children.

Any minor transgression would get you lines. These were usually of the 'I must' or 'I must not' variety, or the totally mystifying 'Hollow objects make most noise'. Fifty times. My hand would ache. Ink from the dip pens covered the page. Ink would be all over my hands and clothes, and my lips and tongue would be blue. Miss Hinchcliffe would stand over us to ensure we did not slack. She would also make multiple attempts to 'correct' my way of writing. I was the only left-hander in the class. Rather than set the paper sideways, allowing me to write easily, she would make me have the paper straight on, cramping me up and making my writing utterly illegible, which would, of course, get me into more trouble.

My school reports were a litany of missed opportunities. My dad never stopped reminding me of the one that referred to 'occasional flashes of brilliance' or the one that said 'if Michael devoted as much time to his work as he does to his role as form clown, his work would improve no end!' Unfortunately, my flashes of brilliance were truly sporadic as I struggled through a fog of incomprehension most of the time. I was dyslexic, a hand-me-down from Dad. I was very slow to read and my 'cack-handed' writing made learning a slow and painful process.

But I loved geography and maps. I would spend hours gazing at the wonders of the world through the pages of the *Reader's Digest Great World Atlas* we had at home. I imagined myself in places I found, both near and far. I longed to travel and in particular I wanted to go to London. So much so that I drew a line on the map from our house to the capital with a Biro and ruler, just to show Mum how easy it as to get there. See! Just one straight road to drive down. Can we go? Awwww, pleeeeease!

The only good thing about being dyslexic was that I got to dodge recorder lessons. These brown plastic instruments were kept in blue plastic sheaths. At the end of each 'music' lesson they had to be dipped in a strong mix of Dettol and water to kill any germs. So next time, they tasted disgusting. My dyslexia robbed me of hand-eye co-ordination; I even struggled to play the first line of 'Three Blind Mice'. Not that anyone noticed above the cacophony of the piano, Miss Hinchcliffe's barked instructions and twenty kids all at different places between the start and end of the tune. I would pretend to blow, hoping the headmistress wouldn't notice. Eventually, I was let off recorder lessons. My struggles with dyslexia meant I was given extra reading and a one-to-one session several times a week – a last ditch effort to get me up to the standard needed for my next school.

My lack of co-ordination made school ball games a trial. I would swish a rounders bat at thin air. In football games I would take up position on the wing, to stay out of the way, and hope nobody passed the ball to me. Any attempt to dribble would end with me tripping over the ball and landing flat on my face; attempts to pass resulted in more swishes at thin air. I was always the last to be picked. But I loved to run and could do it well. I looked forward to sports days if I could just run, without having to carry an egg on a spoon.

In class I would long for playtime and dinner. Lunches were wonderful. We would file into the big hall where tables and chairs had been set out, and line up at Mrs Furness's serving hatch. The food was always hot and tasty and the puddings solid and stodgy, all served with deep yellow custard from huge metal jugs. It was not all brilliant: sometimes we would have sago. We called it frogspawn, because that was what it looked like. I hated it. Sometimes it would be semolina, saved only by strawberry jam, blobbed in the middle and whizzed round until the milk pudding was bright pink. I made the mistake once of telling Mrs Furness she was a better cook than my mum, which she seemed very pleased about. I thought I would tell mum as well. She was less pleased.

Home-time was always a mad rush as we grabbed coats and bags and headed up the hill towards the village. I wanted to get away before a couple of the bigger kids, but they would lie in wait for me by the school gates and tease and push me around all the way to the end of our road. I would arrive home with a torn shirt or skinned knees, with 'specky four eyes' and worse ringing in my ears.

But every morning, it was times tables from two to twelve. Then on through pounds, shillings and pence. After money, we had ounces, pounds and stones, all the way to 'eight stones is one hundredweight and twenty of these to a ton'. We carried on through chains, furlongs and miles, and lastly, bushels and pecks. All this we would enunciate in a monotonous drone, like lines of little robots. This allowed the bigger kids, with the benefit of several years' experience, to be word perfect, and the younger ones to simply move their mouths in the right general direction, uttering not a sound.

19

PIANO SMASHING

When he was younger and considerably more sociable – or just less busy – Dad was a member of Round Table and Mum of the sister organisation called Ladies Circle. Both were founded to do good things for local charities and to have a fun time doing it. Like the Freemasons without all the pompous rituals. While Ladies Circle had coffee mornings and cake sales, Round Table had far more robust ideas for making money, like the annual piano smashing contest.

Because we had a farm and needed to move livestock around, we had a car with a tow bar and, most important, a trailer. So it was Dad's job, along with his pals from Round Table, to collect the old pianos that were destined to meet a messy end. He would travel around West Yorkshire to collect the instruments from people who had no room for them or simply didn't want them any more. Upright pianos had been displaced by the TV or electronic keyboards, both of which took up far less room. Nobody played any more and people would almost pay us to take away their old dark-wood pianos, their keys yellow with age and lack of use. He would load up and deliver them to Hector Buckley's barn.

Pianos had to be fetched from houses, grand and humble. Sometimes three or four beefy men were needed to get the piano up or down some steps or round tight corners. Sometimes the pianos did not get as far as Buckley's barn. One time, we were sent to fetch a piano from near Holmfirth. On arrival we learned it was being stored in an old four-storey woollen mill. On the top floor.

On sight of the instrument, there was a great deal of chin rubbing, head scratching, humming and hawing. There were a lot of stairs. The assembled muscle needed little excuse to leave the piano where it stood, dusty and unloved. Then someone spotted a large loading door. There was bound to be a pulley attached to an arm outside the door. How else would bales of wool have been hoisted to the top?

The door was forced and eventually opened, but there was no pulley system. The effort of opening the door seemed to further reduce the team's resolve. They looked at the door, then at the piano and then at each other, and without a word, the piano was moved at speed, out of the door, accelerating as it hit the ground. The metallic twang echoed off the mill walls and throughout the valley. The piano was in thousands of small pieces and one large one: the cast iron frame was all that remained intact.

Once a year, Buckley's barn was transformed from a cowshed

into an arena, an amphitheatre of destruction, for one night only. Straw bales were stacked all the way around the walls in terraces, to make a mini grandstand. Kids jumped all over the bales, bouncing from top to bottom, the backs of their legs scratched red raw by the prickly straw. There was a barbecue grill laden with sausages and burgers ready to be put in fat white flour-topped baps and stuffed with fried onions and enough ketchup to run down your front when you took a bite.

Around a bar, hastily assembled from wooden planks balanced on stacks of beer barrels, small knots of men drank beer at pace. Piano smashing was likely to be thirsty work and tactics had to be considered. Ladies Circle dished out tea and cake. At one end of the barn a band was setting up. Giant amps were plugged into shiny bright red guitars; drum kits were assembled and loudly tested, making people jump. Tall men with long hair, clad in denim, cowboy boots and attitude, walked the stage, smoking and assembling the entertainment for later. Teenagers stood and stared at the band, transfixed and star-crossed. The place filled with noise, the smell of silage and the cows in the adjacent barn filled the air, mingled with straw, beer, barbecue burgers and excitement.

Each Round Table for miles around had a team, and competition was fierce. There was even a trophy, the past winners engraved on the plinth. Each team of four was armed with a sledgehammer each. The objective was to break down the piano into pieces and feed these through a two foot long, eight-inch-diameter pipe. The team that did this the fastest, won. If you took too long, you were out.

As smashing time approached, the teams would gather, jackets and shirts would be stripped off or sleeves rolled up. To boos and jeers from the other teams, the participants would strut into the straw bale arena like gladiators. The piano seemed to cower in the middle, the men, circling it, stalking it, eyeing it up, assessing any resistance it might offer. Hammers were grasped in mighty arms. Like opening batsmen, the team practised their swings. Warming up, the beer working its brave magic, looking hungry, the team twitched and paced, until a loud whistle sounded and all hell broke loose.

Piano keys flew in all directions and discordant last notes clanged in the bowels of the unfortunate instruments as another hammer blow smashed the keyboard clean in half. The lid was ripped from its hinges and the rest of the shiny mahogany disappeared under a hail of rapid blows. One man would drop his hammer and start to push the remains through the pipe, and soon a tangle of strings emerged from the buckled frame. Splinters of wood continued to fly; blood appeared on arms and faces as they hit home. But still no let up.

Soon all that remained was the metal frame. Now the whole team applied brute force to crack it into bits. Shards of metal flew, kids yelped, women took cover, shielding the smaller kids from the mayhem. The little ones scuttled up the straw-bale steps, out of harm's way.

Then it was over. Big sweaty men in bloodied and torn vests strutted out of the arena, job done, arms aloft. Delirious cheering from their supporter's club was met with loud, good-natured boos from the opposition. The bolder the strut, the noisier the catcalls. The pianos were in thousands of tiny pieces on the barn floor.

Time for more beer. Big bread buns stuffed with burgers now filled the skinned-knuckle hands as the adrenaline-fuelled team warmed down, exchanged banter and compared one another's sledgehammer skills.

When all the teams were done, the prizes would be awarded to more boos and exaggerated cheering. The mess was cleared away and a dance floor was arranged. John and I cringed and our cheeks warmed as Mum and Dad bopped or jived or even twisted, self-consciously at first and then with gusto, as the dance floor filled and the band belted out their set. More beer was drunk; the smell of fried onions filled the night air. We sat on the bales, as high as we could get, fingers crammed in our ears against the blare and thud of the speakers, eyes tightly closed, not daring to look as Dad twisted lower and lower. How embarrassing. The Little Lads would be asleep by now, oblivious to the din, worn out by the excitement and curled up under Mum's coat on the straw bales – lower down, just in case they woke up and rolled off.

Other little kids jigged up and down to the music, out of time, screaming at the assault on all the senses. Others, who had peaked too soon, were draped over their dads' shoulders, thumbs in mouths, eyes screwed shut to keep out the noise. The band played on.

For us, the piano smashing contest was one of the highlights of the year. We got to stay up late, we got to eat burgers – with our hands! – and we got to see the band and after that the fireworks lit up the night sky, leaving their impressions on our tired eyes.

20

CHRISTMAS

It is tempting to say Christmas was like any other day of the year. Animals still needed to be fed and watered and the day started like all the other days of the year with jobs to do on the farm.

When John and I were smaller, there would be time to see what Father Christmas had brought, and for the frantic tearing of paper from tightly wrapped presents and a deep dive into our Christmas stockings that we knew always had some chocolate coins and a precious bright orange satsuma at the very end. But even on Christmas Day, Dad was always keen to be getting on with his jobs, and it was only a sharp glance from Mum that pinned him in place long enough to see us open all our presents.

Mum would have decorated the house. Cards would hang from strings held up with drawing pins along the walls. Lurid red, gold and silver tinsel would deck the tree and long paper chains of red and green spanned the rooms from corner to corner via the light fitting in the middle.

As we grew older and could make ourselves useful around the farm, we would head outside in wellies and duffel coats to help dad get the jobs done more quickly, so he could come indoors and enjoy Christmas Day. It is not certain that we assisted in speeding up anything at all, but at least we were not under Mum's feet as she made a start on Christmas dinner.

Money had always been scarce, and every last penny was invested in the farm. Christmas presents were therefore always very practical: stuff we needed like new socks, a woolly hat or warm gloves. Dad turned his hand to making presents. From the house, we would see the fluorescent yellow glow of the lamp in his workshop as he put his carpentry skills to good use through the dark autumn evenings. One year he crafted a full-sized table tennis table, painting it regulation green. Luckily, Father Christmas had brought us a net, a set of bats and some of the annoyingly fragile little balls. The table was set up in the sitting room. That Christmas we played non-stop, the whole family joining in. We proved, beyond doubt, that as a family we had frankly no hand-eye coordination at all, as most games consisted of wafting the bats into fresh air and trying to retrieve the ball from under the sofa before someone squashed it.

One year he made two wonderful wooden toolboxes for John and me and filled them with woodworking tools. The boxes were painted black, with each joint mitred to fit perfectly. Brass hinges, a stout clasp and a carry handle were added.

The work took hours, but it was done with precision, great care and love. Dad's workshop was perhaps his place to retreat: somewhere that, with a pencil behind his ear and his brow furrowed in concentration, he could be alone with his thoughts, quietly working away.

He had taught himself carpentry with a few visits to night school. Mum had wanted a blanket box, so Dad made one. It was constructed from oak, with each joint carefully drilled and precise wooden pegs fashioned to hold it together. Each panel was stained, varnished and polished to perfection. It sat in the hall at Greetham for decades.

John took to his new tools immediately. He was so like Dad. He watched, he learned, he tried, and in doing so, he developed the practical skills that would become his work. John would take his place in the workshop by Dad's side, a maker and a thinker, a figure-it-out man, a mender, an engineer. He knew exactly what each of the new tools was for and was soon hammering, chiselling and plaining bits of wood into recognisable toys he could play with.

My woodworking attempts usually resulted in bruised thumbs from missed hammer blows, skinned knuckles and cut fingers from slips of the saw blade.

This was a major disappointment to my father, who always valued the practical over the cerebral, engineers and craftsmen over 'paper shufflers' in offices. To this day my brothers have all of the practical skills that seemed to desert me at a very early age.

Dad rendered Christmas day, a normal day. No matter that there would be the largest lunch of the year later on, he would be in for breakfast at his usual time and the usual bacon and egg, toast and tea, which Mum would have ready for him at the time he liked it. After that he would head out again, cap pulled down, collar up round his neck, trousers flapping and wellies slapping, to attend his animals who were of course no respecters of the day either.

If we helped get the farm work done, Dad might just drag himself away in time for elevenses. By this time, a huge turkey would be roasting nicely in the oven and the smells of sage and onion stuffing would be filling the air, along with the savoury fragrance of giblet gravy, bubbling away on the hob. Roast potatoes and parsnips were ready to go in the oven and the long process of boiling the Brussels sprouts to mush was about to begin.

Around midday, Mum might suggest a small glass of sherry for herself. We would take a sip and declare it absolutely disgusting. This was the only 'booze' in the house. It was the same bottle as the year before and the year before that, and probably the only drink Mum had all year. Consequently, it had a disproportionate effect, and she would dissolve into giggles at the slightest prompt and, after only one tiny sherry glass, pronounce herself squiffy. Dad would scowl, half pretending, half genuinely disapproving.

Christmas lunch, like every other lunch of the year, had to be at one o'clock, and Christmas lunch, like every other lunch, would be wolfed down with little ceremony by hungry farmers

149

of all sizes. Completely stuffed, the family would flop drowsily onto the sofa. Dad would fall asleep almost immediately, even Mum would take a short break and for one of very few times a year, the family would be all together around the glowing embers of a coal fire. As if he had a finally tuned internal alarm clock, Dad would snap awake, stretch loudly, and disappear quickly to tend his animals again, just in time to miss the Queen's speech, and unable to resist chastising himself for his idleness.

He might have tried to get his evening jobs done quickly, and he must have felt some kind of small pressure to come in to be with his family on Christmas Day, but if he did, it didn't show. There were always jobs to be done and it seemed likely that Dad fully used the quiet of Christmas Day to get on with one or two additional jobs as well, perhaps trying to compensate for his after-dinner sloth.

Early in the evening, Mum would make a huge pile of turkey sandwiches which would be quickly demolished, as if we had not eaten for days. Slices of sausage meat and stuffing were plated up with rich, crimson cranberry sauce, and cold and claggy clove-scented white sauce. All accompanied by pickles and chopped iceberg lettuce, with tomatoes and cucumber in a huge salad bowl. To follow, there would be left-over Christmas pudding with a huge bowl of trifle, with raspberry jelly, vivid yellow custard and piped cream kisses, all topped off with a sprinkle of multicoloured hundreds and thousands.

We would all sit around the table, chatting, picking the salad plate clean, laughing and joking at one another's expense, until

Sam, with his infectious laugh, would set us all off, and helpless with laughter, we would all collapse, grasping our over-full tummies, until it hurt too much to laugh any more. The banter flowed easily as the brothers took the piss out of one another, exposing weaknesses and focusing on them relentlessly. But nobody ever got upset; we were all well aware of our strengths and weaknesses.

After supper, Dad would press the boys into helping to clear the table, the only day of the year this happened and also the only time he would do the washing up. Plates clattered as we helped to dry and stack. Mum, exhausted and full to the brim with turkey, would usually fall asleep in the chair would and all four of us would squash onto the sofa made for three and squabble while we watched a James Bond film, although Dad always insisted that the plot was 'far-fetched'. Clearly, he had no time for escapism either.

Tidying up the chaos of Christmas would be left for later. Leftovers were carefully set aside for a turkey and ham pie, more sandwiches, even a turkey fricassee for lunch. The turkey seemed to last for days and the carcass would be boiled up with celery, onion and carrots for soup. Nothing was ever wasted.

Christmas presents would still be strewn all over the floor. We would sit surrounded by our new toys, too hot in our new Christmas jumpers in front of the glowing fire. Soon it would be bedtime. Complaints were met with the excuse that we needed to be early to bed because tomorrow was going to be a very busy day with a visit to Granny and Grandad's house, for more presents, more food and another day dictated by the rhythms of farming life.

21

THE RIVER

Scout Dike was the river that ran through our land. Its source was the reservoir of the same name, a drinking water store further up the valley, held in place with steep dam walls. The river cascaded down the dam overflow, the sandstone steps green, shiny and slippery with weed and moss, and through our small valley before emptying into the River Don about two miles downstream. After the cascade and the plunge pool below, the river slowed a little and by the time it passed through our land, it ran gently under the trees either side. The river became our adventure playground.

The water was tinged brown with peat from the moors above the reservoir. The deeper, still parts, under the trees, teemed with large brown trout. Dad reckoned he could tickle trout. By this, he meant standing welly deep in water, very still, gently sliding his hands in and then locking his fingers together under some poor unsuspecting fish. Once in place, the idea was to use the hands to flick the fish up on to the bank. It's a good theory, requiring patience, of which Dad had none.

To his own amazement, he did once manage to flick a fish up on to the bank, but it flapped and squirmed its way back into the water before he could haul his wellies out of the river mud and climb the bank to claim his prize. If we found a long stick, we might tie a string to it and bend a rusty mail to make a hook to go on the end. If we were feeling brave, we might try and dig up a worm and spike it to the hook. We had about as much patience as Dad; the fish remained untroubled.

The river was my escape if I had homework from school or if it was my turn to milk the house cow. The stretches of river upstream from our land ran rapidly, full of energy from the cascade further up. I loved to just stand still, in the water, as the force of the current pressed my wellies to my skin. It was usually too cold in this part of the stream for barefoot paddling, but in places the water was shallow as it tumbled over mossy stones and I could easily walk upstream, from stone to stone. I had read somewhere that deer stand in moving water to massage damaged legs, letting the cold water sooth their torn muscles. I just liked the feel of it, the sound of it and the fact that nobody knew where I was.

The river was set below steep banks and under overhanging trees that in summer made a dark tunnel. The air was filled with the gentle burbles of the water and the rustling of the leaves. Dragonflies flitted around and water boatmen skittered over the surface; the air buzzed. This was one of my secret places.

Downstream, Dad made us a tree house above the river. It was only a few old planks nailed to the thick slimy green boughs of a huge sycamore, but we would take food up there, as well as cushions to sit on and a book to read: *Swallows and Amazons* or a Famous Five. Always competitive, we dropped twigs or leaves into the water and watched them race downstream, betting on whose leaf or stick would be out of sight soonest. Here I could also make myself scarce. I loved my own company. John might be busy on the farm and the two Little Lads were too small to climb the tree, so I often had the tree house to myself. If they wanted to play, they would have to find me first. In summer, when the tree was thick and heavy with leaves, I could hide all day. Dad would cross the river at the shallow ford below me to fetch the house cow for evening milking and not even know I was up there.

Further on, as the river got wider, the banks a bit less steep. Welly-deep in water, my brothers and I started to make our own dam wall, moving the largest, slime-covered green stones that we could carry into place to hold back the water. We would take a spade, cut great sods of earth and plonk them on top. Dad, never one to waste time if automation could shorten a long job, drove a tractor with a loader on the front right up the riverbed, scooping up boulders, large chunks of riverbank, grass, rushes and mud, and made a dam in five minutes flat. The water became satisfyingly deep behind our new dam wall and one day Dad brought home a blue and yellow rubber dingy with a pair of paddles from the camping shop. All four of us rowed up and down the newly deep waters as far as the overhanging trees would let us. We jumped into the freezing stream and played games until our lips were blue with cold.

We were the envy of all our friends.

Then the winter rain came and the stream would run strong. The dam would be flattened until next year, when Dad would get the tractor in the river again and rebuild the dam wall for us. One year the dingy, stored in the shed, was attacked by mice and when we came to get it out in the spring it was full of holes. We improvised with home-made rafts made of anything we could find lying about the farmyard or balancing on wide planks of plywood, cut into a point at one end, surfers on our own water.

Having our own little stretch of river turned our place into a magnet for friends to cool down in the still water behind the dam that Dad built. Summer was a time for the tree house or for borrowing Mum's colander and scooping out great numbers of sticklebacks from the water. I stored them in a huge wooden beer barrel held together with rusty metal hoops. This of course condemned the fish to an early death, as the water got warm quickly and all the oxygen disappeared. Next morning brought a stink of rotten fish and resulted in the barrel being tipped back into the river so the dead ones could float away, perhaps to be consumed by the brown trout in the dark pools under the trees further down.

At the boundary to our land, the stream ran under the blackened sandstone arch of a bridge. Huddersfield Road was about forty feet above the river. Under the bridge it was dark and the water was very still. After it had tumbled over our home-made dam, the water slowed, backed up by another dam downstream. At the far side of the bridge was a rusty steel barrier; bits of dry grass and fine twigs hung from the rails like sheep's wool on barbed wire, showing how high the winter waters had reached. This was as far as I would ever go on my river adventures. In the late afternoon, the sun would catch the barrier and the blocks of concrete that held the rusty red-orange steel in place. But this was where I could hide, under the bridge, away from the hubbub of family and annoying little brothers.

The words on a faded sign just above the high-water mark read 'Trespassers will be Prosecuted' and filled me with a combination of intense curiosity and fear that I might be caught on the next-door farmer's land. The Lord's Prayer, which we droned through at school every morning, says to forgive those who trespass against us. I was not going to take any chances. The farm on the other side belonged to Peter John, who farmed in what my Dad called a 'big way'. I had no intention of trespassing or being prosecuted, and the metal barrier became the limit – as did the depth of the water, now over the top of my boots, one wrong step meaning a very wet foot and a soggy welly for a few days.

22

BONFIRE NIGHTS

A great deal of rubbish accumulated around the farm, and bonfire night was an opportunity to dispose of it. Branches sawn off over-hanging trees, old pallets on which deliveries had been made and any amount of packaging and other rubbish. Dad saw Bonfire Night as an opportunity to have a clear up and burn the lot.

He started to accumulate a pile in the field behind the house, using the loader on the tractor to stack it higher.

As Bonfire Night approached, Mum would be busy in the kitchen making the creamiest toffee. Dad liked the soft creamy variety of toffee rather than the traditional hard and brittle bonfire toffee. Mum also baked parkin, soft moist ginger cake, made with rich, dark bitter-sweet molasses and a Yorkshire Bonfire Night tradition. If we were lucky, we got to lick the sticky spoon. Early in the evening, sausages would be baked in the oven and onions fried ready for the hot-dog rolls.

It became properly dark by late afternoon in November in the Yorkshire hills, and as soon as the jobs were done around the farm, for my brothers and 1, the sense of anticipation would start to grow: a slight feeling of butterflies in the pit of the stomach to start with, soon replaced by full-on excitement as the time to light the fire approached.

Bobble hats would be pulled down over ears and the warmest coats fetched from the back of the cupboard. Friends and neighbours would arrive bearing cake tins full of hot sausage rolls, bonfire toffee and more parkin. Torches would be found from the back of the kitchen cupboards and new batteries inserted. We would shine them into the night sky and watch the pencil thin beams of light criss-cross, in the misty sky before fading into infinity.

Torchlight guided us out of the cosy kitchen, into welly boots lined up by the back door, with thick socks on our feet and our coats tightly buttoned. The wet would make the mud cling to the boots, making them heavy and difficult to walk in. We made our way around the back of the house to the field where the bonfire was ready to light. As impatient as ever, Dad would have a large jerrycan of petrol which he would splash generously over the jumble of wood on the bonfire pile, which by now was usually wet from early November rain.

The petrol guaranteed that the fire would light and he would stand close to the pile with a knot of dry straw in his hand, which he would light before tossing it in the direction of the pyre, igniting the petrol with a dramatic whoomph. The fire caught and with the flames quickly spreading, Dad stepped rapidly backwards, clearly delighted with the fire, now well alight as the rest of the fuel caught, a huge grin on his face, checking his eyebrows had not been singed.

Mum and Dad might have invited farming friends and they usually brought their kids, so there was a lot going on. Friends and family would huddle closer to the fire, feeling its warmth on their faces and hands as the dark night and cold pressed in, the heat from the fire only seeking to exaggerate the cold that still gripped the back of your head and legs away from the flames. The breeze drove the flames higher, bending them over. Dry wood in the middle of the bonfire caught light. Sparks flew into the darkness on the wind, in continuous streams until, cooled by the night air, the tiny lights guttered, leaving only ash to be carried away on the breeze. The air was filled with wood smoke and the fire issued a constant barrage of snaps, crackles and pops.

The kids would edge towards the fire, as if daring to see who could get closest. Hands would be pulled from gloves and out of pockets and held out on straight arms in the direction of the flames. Mittens sewn onto lengths of elastic dangled from the ends of sleeves. Parents exhorted the kids to stand back, but it would not be until something inside the fire collapsed, sending out a plume of new sparks, that we would back-pedal quickly to safety. The grown-ups clustered around the windward side of the bonfire, their happy faces lit by the flames.

Dad was now busy supervising the fireworks. Everyone had brought a box. This was a time before the spectacular public firework displays that are now commonplace. So every firework was given proper attention, wondered at and sometimes even marvelled at, every one lighting a tiny spark of excitement and appreciation. Fire-lit faces turned skywards as rockets fizzed into the night sky, oooohs and aaaaahs greeting the thin explosions and cascades of multicoloured sparks.

Everyone would be full of Bonfire Night food – hot dogs, sweet toffee, and cake – and the children, hyper-active from the sugar and the excitement, now had sparklers. Anxious parents held the hands of the smaller kids, keeping the sparklers away from faces, hands and other kids. We would spin them round in ever faster circles or paint figures of eight in the dark.

By now, the bonfire would be less than half the size as it shrank back around an apron of still-warm grey ash, studded with bright orange embers burning their last. We drew nearer for warmth, the fire no longer hot enough to keep us properly warm; everyone huddled in their coats, pulling hats down to cover chilly ears; cold backs would be turned to the fire, faces to the breeze. The last of the fireworks would be let off with a tame phut. The last rocket, which Dad had saved for an encore, streaked into the sky trailing sparks before cascading streams of gold into the night sky.

We kids would become weary, and the parents grew cold, so people started to drift away, collecting cake tins and leftover food on the way, knocking heavy mud off their wellies and scraping them clean on the grass. Torch lights flicked left to right as everyone walked back to their cars, trailing a stream of thanks to Mum and Dad for their hospitality.

The next morning, a mean wisp of wood smoke would be rising from the remains of the fire, now no more than a rough circle of cooling embers. I would poke at the ashes with a long stick and a flame might pop into life before dying back as suddenly as it had appeared. Soon rain would turn the pile to grey mud that clung like cement to boots. By the spring, grass would be making the fire circle smaller, and by summer it would form a lush circle of dark green. The damp remains of fireworks were strewn around and I would collect them in a bucket, leaving them in the workshop to dry in the hope of extracting some unused gunpowder to make my own fireworks. Burned-out rockets lay out of reach on the roofs of the farm buildings.

23

KILLING TIME

Dad had a growing family to feed, and in the days before our farm shop (by which point we used a local abattoir), that would mean the slaughter of a pig for the new freezer. This was a barbaric spectacle, an assault on all the senses. Killing a pig was an occasion that brought on nerves and that feeling in the pit of the stomach of your guts being squeezed tight by an invisible fist.

Lots of hot water was heated up in a portable boiler, filling the room with steam. The chosen pen would have been washed clean and a block and tackle secured over a solid beam in the roof. It was always a cold night, moonless, dark, when the killing took place. Dad didn't want any interruptions. I suppose it was not strictly legal, and the less anyone saw, the better. Dad had a pistol, black with a short muzzle and sturdy stock, into which he clipped the bullets. The chosen animal would be brought quietly to the pen, at which point John and I would leave, unable to face the actual killing, and

Dad not wanting us to see. No words were spoken; we just made ourselves scarce.

Fascinated, horrified, we waited by the door, part straining to hear the sounds inside that would signal that the deed was done and part not wanting to hear at all. There was no squealing and no loud pistol crack, just a metallic clunk that meant the pig was dead, followed by a calm, respectful and even dignified quiet.

We would peer round the door to see the pig on its side on the concrete, its legs writhing and twitching uncontrollably, a neat red mark in the middle of its forehead and a thin dribble of red blood running across its face. Dad was in his stiff orange rubber apron with the sleeves of his shirt rolled and his cap in place, and a freshly sharp knife already in his hand.

Carefully, Dad would make a nick behind the tendons above the knee joint, one on each back leg. If the pig was still twitching, he asked us to hold its still warm legs while he made the cuts. Into the cut he inserted an iron bar with three indentations in it, one for each leg, and one for the hook on the block and tackle chain. This was attached and the carcass , still twitching as if electrocuted, would be hoisted upwards, the noise of the chain rattling through the block, shattering the calm. Back legs first, the dead animal was now hanging, its snout a foot above the ground, the reflexive writhing now much less.

Dad then made a neat incision: a vertical cut of about six inches in the middle of the throat, causing blood to trickle, and then gush onto the concrete. Vivid reds and maroons spread out across the floor and the lifeblood meandered towards the drain, as the carcass, bled out. Dad checked the hot water and slid the boiler nearer. Dipping a pan, he poured boiling water down the sides of the carcass to scald the skin. Then his quick steel blade expertly scraped the skin clean of coarse hair, which fell to the floor and mixed with the blood that was now starting to cool and clump and run more slowly to the open drain.

Time seemed to stand still; we huddled by the boiler for warmth against the cold night. We were rooted to the spot as Dad, wordless, went about his work. Once he'd cleaned the carcass of hair, he drew a large knife back and forth over a sharpening steel in a quick, easy rhythm. He tested the blade with his thumb, a slight purse of the lips signalling approval, and in seconds a neat slit ran from top to bottom down the centre line of the pig's belly and chest. He opened the body and steam gushed from the still-hot insides, mixing with the steam from the blood and the boiler. The sweet meaty stink was nauseating as the guts spilled towards the ground. Dad expertly severed the connective tissues, stopping as the entire contents of the abdomen and chest cavity were suspended just above the bloody floor.

Next, the valuable bits were separated: metal bowls, ready on the side, were filled with kidneys, liver and heart for the table, and lungs for the dog. When the edible bits had been harvested, the rest was allowed to cascade to the floor in a quivering pile of guts, red and grey and purple and shiny, seemingly constantly on the move. These would be put into a paper feed sack and buried in the muck heap next morning, to rot to nothing for a year or two.

Now Dad carefully applied more boiling water to wash the cavity clean. When the pig was cooler, a few cuts from a sharp cleaver along the line of the backbone would separate the carcass into two halves. The cleaver blows required more force to split the solid skull until the two sides of pork hung limp and flaccid, entirely separate. The whole process took no more than thirty minutes.

In the cold, quiet of the night, the animal was left to hang, and in the dark of the early morning it would be wrapped in a sheet, slung over Dad's shoulders and taken to the kitchen where Mum and Dad, working quickly, jointed, wrapped and put the bits of meat in the freezer. Mum added labels in her neat handwriting. Succulent leg joints for Sunday roast for when visitors came; the shoulders would have the bones removed and then be rolled and tied with string and cut into more joints; the chops carefully cut and packed two by two, Dad scored the skin to make sure we had crackling with our Sunday roast. He took the meat from the head, including the tongue, and all the trimmings went to a butcher friend who would make them into sausages, in return for which he kept half. Nothing went to waste.

With wrapped bits of dead pig still covering the kitchen surfaces, we would sit down to a breakfast of the freshest liver – fried just enough to be slightly bloody and pink – or rich, tender kidneys, with toast to mop the juices, maybe a few mushrooms Dad had picked on his way to see the cattle, a tomato, eggs and some bacon too.

24

MEAT MARKETS

Dad had a way of acquiring skills or at least making things up as he went along in a very convincing way. He applied a little knowledge and made it go a long way. For a man with almost no formal education, he was endlessly practical and learned quickly. His timing with the farm shop was good. It was suddenly a success. The skills that Dad had for rearing a commercial animal that butchers would want to buy meant that the farm produced a steady stream of beef and pork animals of the highest quality and our reputation spread quickly.

We used a local slaughterhouse to process the animals, but the demand soon outstripped the capacity of the farm to supply, so three days a week, a mug of tea balanced on the dashboard of an old van he had bought, he would head out early to Sheffield wholesale meat market. Sometimes he would take me with him. I loved the sights and the sounds of the market: the clatter of commerce.

Even at six in the morning, the market was a buzzing throng of activity. The salesmen chattered as they engaged their buyers or shouted instructions to the porters. The market was adjacent to the slaughterhouse, a huge commercial meat factory where lorry loads of cattle, sheep and pigs from all over the district were offloaded to the lairage before being herded to the killing halls; within hours they were dead, chilled and ready for sale the next day. The market area was vast, made up of stands occupied by the wholesalers. Every type of meat and offal was on display, freshly dead and with specks of blood dripping onto the sawdust covering the red-painted floors.

Those still half-asleep, like me, lingering in the way, would be loudly cursed by burly and bloodied meat porters, their white overalls shiny with grease from carrying meat from the market to waiting trucks on their broad shoulders. Even their little white peaked caps were blood stained. Huge sides of beef hung in rows from hooks that were attached to rollers that ran the length and breadth of the market. This way, carcasses were moved around and onto the wholesalers' stands for sale.

Here, the sides of beef would be quartered with, razor-sharp knives, or separated into whole rumps or sirloins with rapid cuts and quick movements of sharp saws. Once the buyers had made their choice, strong men carried the fore and hind quarters to the weighing scales for a chitty to be written with the weight and the agreed price.

The wholesalers knew every trick. One would engage you in deep discussion, all the time resting his pint pot of strong tea on the scales, adding a few pounds to the weight of the beef and quickly noting it on the ticket before you noticed. A sturdy metal meat hook might also be weighed. A good operator sold the hook and mug of tea many times a week, always at the price of prime beef. Once the buying was done, it was time to settle up. The wholesalers' offices were havens of calm as lightening quick hands pressed calculator buttons and added up the chits before money quickly changed hands.

In the market, Dad came alive, all his senses on the lookout for a deal. He would be uncharacteristically full of banter and chat with his preferred suppliers; always keen to get a bargain, he would haggle with the salesmen for the best prices, his knowledge of the market seemingly endless. He would smile and chat and pass the time in a way I had never seen him do before: he was in his element. He knew the quality his customers wanted, and he knew how much he was going to pay for it.

He could tell how long the beef had been hung by the quality of the fat on the carcass. He wanted matured beef for its tenderness, not something freshly dead, and he didn't want to have it taking up space in his fridge for a couple of weeks before he could sell it. Quite prepared to turn his back and walk away if the prices didn't suit him, nine times out of ten the salesman would have a re-think and come scurrying after him. Dad paid cash, didn't need credit and that type of customer needed to be taken seriously. He said he always bought at better prices for cash.

When the deals were done, the porters would load the van, and we moved on to buy lamb. Still frozen solid from the boat trip from New Zealand and a ghostly white, they were wrapped in muslin cloths to avoid freezer burn. They remained frozen all the way home and were just ready to be cut into joints on Dad's band-saw. In season, fresh English lambs, the carcasses pink and plump, were bought and taken home to cut and wrap. We would buy pork bellies or pig's heads from which we would strip the meat to make our special recipe sausages.

As soon as I could drive, I would take on the morning trip to the market by myself. I would have a list of what to buy. I was blissfully unaware that Dad had warned the wholesalers that if they sold 'the lad' any rubbish he would bring it back the next day and personally ram it down their throats. So I was greeted with mock respect: lots of 'Yes, of course, Mr Kirby!' and 'What else can we do for you today, young sir?' I knew they were 'extracting the Michael' as Dad would say, when he really meant taking the piss.

I leaned fast and Dad never had to take anything I'd bought back. None of this stopped the salesmen trying to interest me in some mummy lambs for example – sales speak for tough old ewes, only fit for curried mutton. One even tried to interest me in a case of linnets' tongues. Only once did I come unstuck, buying a job lot of cheap pork bellies that I planned to make into sausages. Mum and Dad were away for a couple of days, and I soon realised I had bitten off more than I could chew. I spent most of one night taking the meat off the bones and preparing the sausage mix. As I dug into the pile, I found the ones near the bottom were turning green and slimy and starting to smell. I binned these and the bone man collected them before Dad got back. I said nothing and neither did he, but it was a lesson learned. As he might say, "nuff said'.

25

FARM WORK

Helping with the farm work was not only an expectation, it was also, often, a necessity. Dad's relationship with schooling meant that, in his mind, academic work was always a poor second to getting things done around the farm.

Most of my friends at school who were sons of farmers felt the same burden of expectation from their own fathers, and all of them worked the farm with their dads. Perhaps there was an expectation that this was an investment in their future, that maybe one day they would inherit the farm – but until that day, they had to earn it.

At our house, sitting around for any length of time at all was never going to be an option. Dad would wonder aloud what people with 'proper jobs', who finished at five, did until bedtime. Sitting around watching television was beyond his understanding. Consequently, while television was not exactly rationed, we weren't allowed to watch endless hours of what Dad dismissed as rubbish. Mondays at nine was a rare exception. We were allowed to watch *Alias Smith and Jones* and stay up until ten.

The necessity to have everyone muck in was brought on by the economics of farming. My brothers and I sometimes worked together, for instance when stock needed moving, but usually we had our own individual jobs, our differing skills creating a clear division of labour. While I would be busy in the shop, John or Andy might be driving tractors, John was far handier with a tractor. I retained my early fears of farm machinery. He was practical, had learned to fix pretty much anything and was starting to gain some of my Dad's extra senses around the livestock. Sam might help Dad move animals around or muck out. This way we grew up working together but separately; rarely were two people needed for a job, so we just got on with the ones we had.

Making money was, as ever, cyclical. It was possible to make money farming, and it was possible to lose money too. A run of bad luck, the loss of a good milk cow or a tractor engine blowing up could mean cash got very tight. In the good times we could employ casual labour or even a professional stockman, although these outsiders never lasted long. Dad had his own ways of doing things and it was usually a case of 'my way or the highway'. Anyone lacking his innate ability to understand animals – i.e. everyone – was always going to fall short.

So my brothers and I would be pressed into farm work at various stages of the day, usually after school when homework would be put on hold. Our parents had few expectations for us when it came to school. Mum claimed we succeeded in life despite school. Mum and Dad never pushed us. Perhaps they just didn't think it was important.

All four of us probably lived down to their expectations academically. We all struggled at school, all showing signs of dyslexia to a greater or lesser extent. This left us with a legacy of always having to play catch-up in life, of being labelled as not very bright, just like our Dad. But from both our parents we acquired a confidence, an innate sense that with hard work and what Dad always referred to as 'application' we would indeed turn out all right, that we would 'do OK'.

The hard graft of farm work, often cold, wet, encrusted with mud and sometimes worse, gave all of us very a clear – priceless – set of values: that nothing ever came for free, that anything worth having was worth working for. So we recorded our hours, we put in our weekly time sheets and we were paid for our work

When we were short-handed on the farm, John would be carting muck or slurry spreading and I would be employed in the farm buildings. Mucking out was a never-ending task with the pig unit, where we came to house hundreds of greedy, shitting animals, whose toilet habits I came to despise. This involved scraping the soiled bedding and excrement into the dark passageways that ran behind the pens, and with the help of lots of water, moving huge volumes of crap towards the drains where gravity would take over moving the muck down into the holding tanks so that John could suck it back out again with his tractor and vacuum tanker and spread it on the fields. The concentrated smell of the effluent made your eyes water. The smell stuck to your hair and clothes and seemed impossible to wash off, no matter how many times you tried.

We would also do the feeding round. Large-wheeled trolleys containing the feed would be trundled from the milling and mixing machine up and down the feeding passages. At feeding time, the noise would be deafening as hundreds of animals complained loudly about the slow progress made in bringing their dinner. Once fed and mucked out, the pigs had to be given clean sawdust bedding: a dusty, itchy job.

In a drive to be as efficient as possible, much of the concentrated pig feed that we used was milled and mixed at home. This was years ahead of its time; most farmers still bought in ready-made feeds from specialist animal-feed mills. Dad worked out what these mixtures contained and decided he could do things better and have more control over the animals' diet, at less cost, if we did it ourselves. We bought grain to feed the milling machine and concentrated protein such as fish meal or soya would be tipped into the mix along with a pre-prepared blend of vitamins and minerals. This way we produced several tons of feed in one go.

At weekends, if there were any litters of week-old pigs that needed injections. Dad would press-gang whichever son was around to catch and hold the piglets still long enough to inject them with an iron solution, against piglet anaemia, the mother's milk containing insufficient iron to enable them to thrive.

Dad was meticulous about controlling disease. He knew from his bitter experience of the foot-and-mouth outbreak just how quickly a virus could spread through a herd. When a pen of pigs was vacated it would be washed out and thoroughly disinfected before fresh bedding and a new group of pigs were brought in. Washing out was not challenging work and would allow plenty of time for daydreaming. Unfortunately, sometimes this meant that things got sprayed that did not mix well with water, like the plug sockets for the heat lamps. Giving these a quick accidental spray would plunge the whole farm into darkness, certain to have Dad cursing loudly as he tried to remember what he had done with the torch so he could find the junction box and repair the damage.

On a visit to Denmark – his first time on an aeroplane and first time out of the country – Dad had seen early versions of sow stalls. Sows tend to be territorial and can fight, often wounding each other. Housing the sows in long lines of stalls was seen as a sensible solution at that time. This meant that the animals had to be tethered with chains around their necks. Dad made special halters with tubes to prevent the chains from rubbing. The chains were fixed into the concrete on the floor of the stalls which were around four feet wide. A trough at the front provided a place to eat, and the manure was collected behind the animal in a convenient passage ready for scraping down the hole and into a waste tank.

Before the stalls, the sows had been used to living in groups in loose boxes and they hated the restrictions on their freedom of movement that the stalls brought. The halters would be around their necks just behind their jaw bones and impossible to escape from: they weren't happy. Initially they would struggle violently against the tethers before eventually settling down into extremely dull routine involving two feeds a day. Bored animals would slowly grind their teeth on the chains, over time wearing the links thin with the constant chewing. That stalls were inhumane never really occurred to us or any of the other thousands of farmers who kept pigs in this way. At that time there was little or no public consciousness about the treatment of animals on farms and farming methods like this made good economic sense. The animals were warm and well fed, they had dry bedding every day and fighting was eliminated completely.

The farming day was always a dawn-to-dusk affair. With animals, there was never any respite. Pregnant mothers are no respecters of the clock when it came to giving birth. Animals needed feeding both ends of the day, every day of the year. To people who didn't really understand farming, the day in, day out routine of milking or feeding might be seen as monotonous and boring. But the daily routines are overlaid with weekly routines, and these in turn by seasonal changes. Most days bring new life end every day brings the opportunity to see your animals growing and thriving. Every day is different.

Outside in the open air, the intensity of light, the direction and the strength of the breeze, or the hammering of the rain on asbestos roofs make every day unique if you only pause to notice. Once the routines of milking or feeding or mucking out are done, the variety of other jobs that need doing is endless, whether that is the hectic rush of harvest time, the contemplative pleasure of rebuilding a drystone wall, laying a hedge to make it stock proof or mending a length of fence.

Huge satisfaction comes from taking your best animals to market and realising a good price, or having a fine day when you can finally finish the roof off on the new barn, or even just a hard frosty morning that means you can get on the land without churning it up.

An uncompromising approach is required to get everything done that needs to be done daily and still make progress on the things that will help build a stronger and more resilient farming enterprise for the future. Successful farmers need drive and energy and the motivation not only to survive but to improve and grow and develop. Both of our parents were lucky enough to have all these things, and their sons were lucky enough to inherit them.

26

DONNY MARKET

Saturday was market day in Doncaster. Back then the stock-yards down by the side of the River Don were full of movement and noise. Huge lorries with three decks of sheep, down from the hills, jostled with Land Rovers and trailers in the queue for an unloading bay. Sheep, cattle and pigs were disgorged down steep ramps into galvanised steel pens. The lorry drivers shouted, wielding sticks and even electric cattle prods to get their trucks unloaded so they could park up for a big breakfast from the market café and a snooze before the repeat process at the end of the market.

Hooves rumbled on the ramps and the gates to the pens banged shut, clanging like discordant bells. Loud noises from dislocated sheep and cattle filled the air and the farmers and dealers, buyers and sellers, leaned against the pens, smoking and chatting and running critical eyes over the stock. The place smelled of straw and disinfectant and the air was filled with expectation.

We would load up early and be on the road by 7. Dad would have his mug of tea on the dashboard. Mum would make us bacon sandwiches with ketchup or brown sauce in soft white floury baps, wrapped in greaseproof paper for later. These rarely survived longer than it took to leave the village before we wolfed them down. We would skirt Barnsley before pulling up the steep hill to Wath, Goldthorpe, Hickleton and into Doncaster. The car would get hot with the effort of pulling the trailer.

Doncaster was prosperous in those days. Miners' families rich with payday cash would be in town from the surrounding pit villages. It had a new shopping mall, the Arndale Centre. This was quite famous, as the planners had decided that a huge statue of a naked couple, standing, hips pressed tight together and arms stretched joyfully skyward, was just what a post-industrial northern town needed to brighten the place up.

The statue proved just too fascinating for a pre-pubescent boy and, when I was old enough to go into town by myself, a trip to the Arndale was a guilty must, though I never mentioned this to my dad. The figures had been there, having sex, for ages and nobody who lived in Donny cared any more. Years later, the statue, apparently called *The Lovers* was moved to grace a plinth in a run-down suburban shopping precinct.

Doncaster had a huge pig market where store pigs (young animals that would be sold to farmers who would grow them on), porkers, bacon-weight pigs and cull sows sold in their thousands. Before we had the farm shop, we would take store pigs in most Saturdays. We would back carefully up to the ramp and let the trailer door down. Next to us was either a huge lorry with a hundred pigs on board, or, on one occasion, a farmer unloading half a dozen store pigs from the back seat of a dark purple Rover 3000, shit everywhere on the carpets and leather upholstery.

The sale of the pigs would begin at 10.30. It might be noon before they got to our lot. Dad wanted his pigs penned in the best place. Not too early in the sale, so the buyers were nicely warmed up – but not too late, as they might have got their truck-full already.

The market was a place to meet farming colleagues. Dad knew some of them from his work with the ministry but because of his disdain for small talk, once we dropped the pigs off and saw them safely penned, we hustled into town, usually on some mission or other.

Doncaster had a large indoor and outdoor market, selling everything. Stalls loaded with fruit and veg vied for attention with those selling pillows or toys. Trucks selling hot dogs were packed tight with fridge lorries selling freezer packs of meat. The shouts of the market men were loud and persistent. The crockery man would balance a complete bone- china tea service on his arm, heaving it in the air with a clatter to show how durable the pieces were, all the while telling people he wasn't going to let them pay £20 or even £10, they could have the lot for a fiver. He always drew a crowd with his patter and his juggling skills, and his tea sets sold like hot cakes. Dad might need to get some supplies for the farm, or he might get distracted by a whole fresh pineapple or something equally rare he could take home to Mum. We both loved the hubbub of the market and with time to kill, it was one of the few times Dad's pace slackened.

Beyond the market was the town centre. One time, Dad, needing a present for Mum's birthday, ventured into British Home Stores, the underwear department to be precise.

'Here, take this,' he said urgently as he pressed a tenner into my hand and pushed me forward.

'Go on, take these to the till.' He paused to pick a bra-and-pants set from the racks, pressing this too into my hand and propelling me firmly towards the pay desk, unnecessarily quickly. When I took my place in the queue, I turned to find him gone, peering furtively over some shelves at a safe distance. By now I was trapped. I stared at my feet, not knowing where else to look. My embarrassment was total; my cheeks burned bright red as I stood waiting to pay, wishing the earth would swallow me whole. He just smirked.

When I was a bit older, Dad would let me go into town by myself, and after a quick peek at the naked couple in the Arndale, I would visit the bike shop at the far end of the high street. I needed to see 'my' bike. To be precise, a metallic brown Raleigh Mercury race bike with subtle diamond-bright 'world champion' rainbow rings on the downtube. I would stare at it, my nose pressed hard to the glass of the front window, needing it so much, it hurt. I want back every Saturday to make sure it was still in the window. I was saving like mad. When I was eleven, Dad paid me eleven pence an hour, but only if I filled in my weekly time sheet. A birthday meant a pay rise.

It took quite a while to save up, but with my pay from the farm and a bit of birthday money, I was getting close. My account at the Leek and Westbourne building Society was swelling slowly with interest earned. Every time we were at the market, I would run to the shop, praying my bike was still there. Until, one day, it wasn't. My heart broke. I think I almost cried. Could it be inside? I had never dared to actually *go* into the shop. Dad thought going into shops meant they might try and sell you things. I stepped through the door. 'Can I help you, son,' asked a man in a brown coat. 'Just looking, thank you,' I told him, avoiding eye contact, scared stiff I was about to be sold something. Close to panic, I urgently scanned the rows of bikes inside. My bike was still in the shop, lined up with some others at the back. I breathed again and fled.

Eventually I had the money I needed to buy the bike, I walked in, head up, heart racing, palms clammy with anticipation, and told the man in the brown coat that I wanted to buy *that* one please, and please could I ride it out of the shop, right now, please. Thank you. I had waited for ever for this. My life was complete. The man lifted the bike down for me and I laid my hands on it for the first time, immediately lifting it up, not really believing that it could be so light.

I had told Dad I wanted to ride it home, and so I did. At least as far as the first big hill, when I stopped at a phone box, exhausted, backside sore from the bone-hard saddle, and called for rescue.

At the market, the sale of store pigs was starting. A man with a large hand bell summoned a crowd. The auctioneer barked 'pig buyers' above the noise of the animals and people. A large knot of buyers moved down the lines of pens, while the auctioneer and his clipboard man walked along the planking above them, looking down on the audience.

Geoff Spinks was the auctioneer, a tall, authoritative man with jet-black hair and a deep baritone voice. Immaculate in his jacket and tie and polished market boots, he stood apart. He had huge presence that seemed to fill the high-roofed market hall and rise effortlessly above the noise at his feet. His patter was fast and efficient. He would know instinctively when his buyers had reached the top of the bids and he would sell the pens quickly with a loud cry of 'All done now, sold!' His long stick, his gavel, crashed hard and loud against the metal pens before being pointed at the buyer. The clipboard man would take a note and Geoff would already be moving to the next pen. Of all the auctioneers in the market, Dad was convinced Geoff got us the best prices.

I wanted to *be* Geoff Spinks so much. His authority was complete as he controlled his crowd as well as any rock star. He towered over the market. I would be at the front of the group that followed him, pressed hard against the metal rails. My excitement would grow as we got near to our pens. Dad was justifiably proud of his livestock. We wanted to see them make a good price, and I would glow with pride if Geoff said some good words about our pigs before starting off the bidding process.

I would never be able to see who was bidding. How Geoff picked out the bids was a real art. He knew all the buyers and their little ticks, nods, winks, jerks of the head or slight raises of a chin or eyebrow that signalled a bid. Years later, I would accompany Dad buying cattle from another market. He would get right up next to the auctioneers stand and reach round, tapping the auctioneer's leg each time he wanted to bid. Importantly for Dad, nobody knew he was bidding. What the auctioneer thought of being touched up like this is not recorded.

The sale complete, I would get to take the chit to the market office and collect what seemed to me to be a big bundle of ten- and twenty-pound notes. I would watch as the tellers, licking their thumbs, counted the piles of notes at lightning speed before handing the money over to me. The next task was to take a crisp twenty and, finding the buyer of our pigs, press the money into his hand 'for luck'. We had some loyal buyers for our stock, and we wanted to keep them sweet. I missed Donny Market when we didn't go any more.

Before home-time, Dad would buy a cup of tea at the market café, a large room in a corner, off the market hall. Here the smells of the market mingled with the acrid smoke of a hot plate, covered with bacon, sausages, fried eggs and black pudding, as well as yellowing slices of fried bread which mopped up the fat and the flavour. Boiling kettles for endless cups of tea caused a smoggy emulsion of steam and cigarette smoke to fill the room. The walls dripped with condensation. The loud bray of farmers swapping market tales was deafening.

Outside, huge lorries were being loaded in a reverse of the early-morning process. Large, rough men would wave sticks at confused animals, driving them up steep ramps into the trucks, with a combination of big sticks, electric cattle prods and foul language.

The market was a place of noise and movement, exciting and exhausting. We would wend our way home, weary. Dad would usually be pleased and chatty about the good trade, certain our pigs were the best for sale that day, another wedge of notes secure in his inside pocket.

The pineapple would be presented to Mum as a great prize when we got home. I still preferred the ones that came in tins though.

27

SMELLS

As the number of animals at the pig unit at Scout Dike increased, so the question of effluent started to loom large in my life.

The farm was only four hundred yards from our school gates. On days when the wind was blowing in the wrong direction or if Dad was spreading slurry on nearby fields, the smell of pig manure would seep inexorably into every corridor and classroom. The school was populated by kids from the local towns and a fair number of farmers' kids like us. It was located on the edge of open countryside; the surrounding farming was there for all to see. But quite often, the teachers would close the windows, usually too late, trapping the smell of fresh pig slurry inside, rather than keeping it out.

I could feel myself visibly shrink on muck-spreading days, desperately wanting to disappear. Scared stiff that the penny would drop and the whole class would turn to me because of the smell, I thought I could feel the eyes staring accusingly at my back. I couldn't help reddening, overwhelmed by that hot itchiness that comes with acute embarrassment. I knew full well that it was our farm that was the culprit and I self-consciously imagined that the other kids did too. I would stay silent and feign ignorance. If the stink was mentioned, I'd hold my nose as if I was just as bothered about the smell as everyone else, like I'd dropped a huge fart and was pretending it wasn't me.

We had too much slurry to spread on our own fields. But local farmers placed a very high value on the effect our particular brand of farmyard manure had when you spread it on the grass fields. Every time someone sniffed the air, or let out an exclamation, usually regarding the strong smell of shit, I would long for the ground to open up and swallow me whole. To make matters worse, sometimes Dad would drive his tractor and slurry tanker past the school as he ferried muck to some neighbouring field, and I could no longer pretend it was nothing to do with me.

My immediate friends were mainly farmers' sons, but their farms were further away. None of the guilt attached to them and they provided me with no defence, sometimes being the first to point out the source of the stink, making sure they didn't get the blame. I would have to hide at break time, pretending I needed to go to the library or shutting myself in the boys' toilets so I didn't have to go outside.

Worse still was the tendency of the slurry tanker that was towed behind a tractor to leak unspeakable liquids onto the road that passed right by the school gate. Multiple trips would lead to a slow but pungent build-up of muck on the road, which Dad was keen not to bring to the attention of the local constabulary. The tractor tyres, heavy with mud from the fields, trailed even more filth onto the tarmac.

Totally oblivious to the embarrassment this would cause, after school, Dad would dispatch me up the lane and onto the road with a three-foot-wide squeegee to scrape what I could into the gutter so the next rain could wash it away. Perhaps he thought doing jobs like this would make me stronger, more resilient, more humble even. That is, if he ever thought about this task like that at all. He probably just saw a mess that needed to be cleared up.

Straight after school, the skinny kid in smelly work clothes and wellingtons would be scraping the lumpy brown liquid into the gutter, just as the school buses were slowly passing by and people were leaving late from school, walking down the footpath with their noses pinched tight, taking every advantage of my embarrassment. My humiliation was complete.

28

MOTORS

When the penny dropped with Dad that none of his lads were really the slightest bit interested in being the next champion showjumper, or indeed ever getting on the back of something that big that had a mind of its own, the horses had to go. We needed the steep field on the opposite side of the river to ride our motorbikes round.

We always seemed to have a motorbike at the back of a shed somewhere, ignored and gathering dust until, out of the blue, Dad would decide that it was time to pull it out and feel the wind in his hair. He would unscrew the spark plug and give it a quick clean with a wire brush, and then syphon a bit of petrol out of one of the cars and pop a bit in the tank, before doing something he called priming the carburettor. Most of the time none of these things worked, but he would push the motorbike down the lane assisted by as many small boys as he could muster, before dropping the clutch and winding the throttle back, hoping that the back wheel would bite and that the engine would fire up.

Eventually, breathless and sweaty from pushing, the motorbike would either be parked back in the shed so we could have another go, another day, or the spanners would come out and pretty soon bits of motorbike were strewn across the floor. Occasionally the engine would fire, Dad would leap aboard and – to his obvious delight – be off down the lane, throttle wide open, cap turned backwards, a big daft grin spreading over his face. There was nothing like riding motorbikes to get the adrenaline flowing.

The first bike he acquired was an old Honda 90. The owner had broken down on the road that ran past the farm and he pushed the bike up to the house and asked if he could keep it in one of our buildings until he had time to come back and get it. Dad said yes, of course he could, but the man never came back. After a decent amount of time had passed, Dad assumed that it was OK to see if the bike would start. He fiddled with it a bit and got it going. Still nobody showed up to collect it, so perhaps a bit of a blast down the lane or even around the fields might be fun.

Clearly motorbikes were just as much fun as horses. We would take it in turns to ride pillion, arms stretched around his waist, holding on tightly as he jolted and bucked over the bumpy farm tracks. Our hands shook and legs trembled, literally weak at the knees with the thrill of it all.

The Honda 90 was a machine built for sedate commuting on the roads, and it was certainly not designed for belting around farmers' fields, and gradually bits started to fall off it, or were removed in the interests of lightness and speed. In our minds we had a stripped-down racing machine. When the 'left-behind' bike finally gave up the ghost, it was replaced by a succession of similar ones, usually cheap and well past their best, and we would career round the fields making worn tracks in the grass as we lapped the steep embankments.

Eventually, we got our first proper motocross bike, a full-sized 250cc brute of a machine, just a bit too big for me to touch the ground either side to start with, and certainly too powerful for my skinny arms and limited courage. It was lightning quick. If you twisted the throttle too hard, the front wheel would rear up and deposit you, off the back, on the base of your spine. The adrenaline rush was unsurpassed. We were lucky to have fields to ride around, and the same kids who sneered at me from the school buses now looked enviously out the windows as I sprinted home from school, quickly changed into my work clothes and blasted up and down the fields on my motorbike as they went by.

Dad was skilful and fearless and would always want a go. He would career down the hill at full speed, flat cap on backwards so it didn't lift off in the wind (no thought of a helmet). One time the throttle stuck open, and the only way to stop was to press hard on the back brake and lean the bike onto its side. Both Dad and bike slid into the wall at the bottom of the hill, the only damage a bent brake lever and Dad's bruised ego. He climbed to his feet, a sheepish grin on his face, telling us not to tell Mum. As we grew and moved on, we handed our motorbikes down to the Little Lads, who grew to love riding them too. But Dad was always keen to prolong our love affair with bikes and would take us to Sheffield Speedway.

Held at Owlerton Stadium, it became a weekly fixture: every Thursday in the summer we would be there without fail. A rainy-night postponement of a fixture left us despondent.

Even today, I vividly recall the noise, the smells and the excitement of Speedway night. I cannot smell freshly baked bread without thinking of Thursdays. I cannot think of fish and chips without being back to those nights out in Sheffield. If a motorbike goes by, the exhaust smell takes me back to climbing the fence of the pit lane to get a better view.

We would always try to get there early but rarely managed it. Dad always wanted to park the car facing home, never in the official car parks with the queues to get in and out and the charges for the privilege. We would join the regulars heading to the stadium. When we were younger, Dad would press me and John through the turnstile together to get us both in for the price of one. His argument was that we were only small. It sometimes worked.

As soon as we were in, we needed to head to the pits. John and I would worm our way through the forest of legs to the wire mesh fence that kept the riders apart from the spectators. The riders would be making their way in, leather clad, signing autographs on match programmes for the kids. In the pits, the Speedway bikes would be lined up on stands, facing the wall, back wheels four inches from the floor. With single cylinder 500cc engines, no brakes and no silencers, the bikes were lean, stripped down for speed. The home team, our team, Sheffield Tigers, were to the left and the away team lined up their bikes on the right. Our arch rivals were the Halifax Dukes and Bell Vue Aces from Manchester. These matches drew bigger crowds and noisy, partisan fans. The tension mounted as the riders joined their machines.

The warm-up would begin. A mechanic in oily overalls approached each bike, turned the fuel line to 'on' and grasped the rear wheel tight, spinning it against the resistance of the engine until it fired up. The noise was deafening and the deep-throated roar of the bikes filled the night air and reverberated in your chest. The heady smell of Castrol R engine oil billowed out over the pits. We would breathe in the night air, filled with these sweet fumes. If the bikes were slow to start, they would be bump started by the riders down the ramp to the track, then they would roar back into the pits, riding side saddle with their hair blowing behind them.

Our favourite riders would stand by their bikes with one hand on the throttle, the other on their hip. They were insouciant, cool and showed no sign of the nerves we felt, smoking as they shouted to teammates or mechanics above the din of a dozen revving engines. As they built the revs up, blipping the throttle, they would rest their hands on the cylinder head to take the pulse of their machines. They wore leathers with sponsors' names attached, rolled down to the waist on warm evenings.

Before the first race, we would make our way to track side. Our seats were just in front of the start line. The track was a four-hundred-yard oval. At Owlerton, it was made of dark red shale. The anticipation built as a round man in a brown suit with a red face and a tanned bald head sat astride a blue Fergie tractor and started the process of preparing the track for the racing to come. The wheels of the bikes threw the shale to the outside of the track and this man's job was to re-distribute it evenly again. He would do multiple laps and the smell of the diesel fumes from his tractor drifted across the stadium, mingling with the irresistible smell of fried onions from the hot-dog sellers and the beery breath of the crowd.

The start gate was three strands of elastic tape stretched between two posts. When the tapes went up, the riders roared forward, throwing great plumes of grit behind them, ready for the tractor man to re-grade again between races.

Dad always sat next to Harry Bufton, a successful businessman who he had known since he was a kid. Harry sponsored Reg Wilson, a small, muscular, tanned racer with long blond rock-star locks. Wild and inconsistent, Harry would curse Reg loudly or bask in reflected glory, depending on how he was doing. Harry said Reg was thick and never listened, but he still provided Reg with the best equipment in return for Reg carrying Harry's company name on his leathers. If Reg hit the deck, Harry seemed more concerned about the bikes he had paid for than Reg's well-being.

Our best rider was Dougie Wyer. Doug was very fast and Harry would tell everyone in earshot that he'd sponsored the wrong rider, but I think he liked the mantle of long-suffering mentor of the glamour-boy of Sheffield Tigers.

Dad would get emotionally involved in the racing, showing a passion that rarely surfaced anywhere else. If the racing was close and the points on offer needed to win the match, along with everyone in the stand, he would rise to his feet, bellowing at the top of his voice to 'C'mon!' and punching the air, and if the results went our way, actually jumping up and down with his arms aloft, smiling broadly.

To my teenage brothers and me, too self-conscious to throw ourselves into the emotion of the occasion, Dad was just plain embarrassing. During the racing, he would be tense and displayed nerves that never surfaced elsewhere. He would be visibly moved by the bravery of the riders. If there was an accident, he would fall silent. He would join the ripple of respectful, relieved applause as an injured rider got to his feet or had to be stretchered off. If there was a nasty crash or a rider hurt on the track, Dad would be obviously upset.

The summer sun would set behind the stands and the track lights would shine brightly, the atmosphere building as the dark closed in, the track an oasis of light. The stadium lights were dimmed just before the start of each race. The crowd would fall silent as the riders approached the start gate, before erupting as the tapes went up and the bikes roared into the first corner. The echo of the engines bounced like distant thunder off the surrounding hills, seeming to multiply. But too soon, the racing was over. The league match was settled, the home crowd either ecstatic or broken.

We would try and make a move early to miss the traffic. Dad would hustle us towards the big exit gates and start to run. This

196

soon became a sprint down the middle of the road, dodging the few cars. On our right was the Sunblest Bakery, makers of the soft white sliced loaves that were our staple at home. Huge extractor fans blew warm air from the ovens, laden with fresh bread smells into the night air. Dad, always competitive, was determined to be first back to the car and we would trail back, breathless, hot and exhilarated from running flat out. He would have the car doors open and we would pile in and be away in seconds, laughing out loud between gasps for air. We were first out of the stadium, first to be on our way home, the fastest and the smartest, the headlights of the stadium traffic mere dots in our rear-view mirror.

There was method in all that Dad did. The car was parked facing home for a reason. There was no point in losing our advantage by having to do a U-turn, and we had to be at the chip shop before the rest of the Speedway crowd or we would have to queue.

John and I would jump out of the car to be first into the chippy. Three lots of chips, salt and lashings of vinegar, and little scraps of crispy batter, hot from the fryer, on top, all folded into a greaseproof square of paper and wrapped tight with yesterday's *Sheffield Star and News*. Back in the car, we'd be eating chips in the dark as Dad drove, loading hot chips into his mouth with his fingers.

When we arrived home, full of chips, the adrenaline rush of the Speedway and the sprint to the car was not enough to keep us awake any longer, and with the sounds of the track still ringing in our ears, we fell asleep as soon as our heads hit the pillow.

We continued to ride our motorbikes. John graduated to cars and had an old red Mini that he would drive around the farm, learning to drive long before he passed his driving test. Dad got older and more sensible: no more power slides or using drystone walls to stop.

29

GRAPPLE FANS

Dad, my brothers and I loved wrestling (Mum not so much), and *World of Sport* was one of the few things we would watch together on TV. Dickie Davies, with his quiff, moustache, kipper tie and huge lapels, would introduce the action. It was rare for Dad to sit still long enough to watch a whole hour of television, but on Saturday afternoons at four p.m., the animals would have to wait for their evening feed. We would gather round the telly to see who was fighting this week. Mum would be hiding behind the Saturday paper, glad of a bit of a sit, as we waited for the MC to announce the fighters.

When we were young and naive, we thought the fighting was for real. As we got older it became clear that this elaborately choreographed 'sport' was nothing like real sport at all. It was a pure entertainment: a theatre with a raised square stage, bounded by ropes, with finely drawn characters – heroes and villains, pretty boys and man mountains, thugs whose only weapon was a forearm smash and artists whose movements flowed liked ballet.

It was introduced by Kent Walton, who had the grace to go along with the comedy and tragedy played out in the ring; he kept it authentic and provided an expert running commentary on fighters' brutal and athletic moves. Dad would scoff at the antics of some of the fighters, calling the fights 'put-up jobs', but he would still be glued to the telly until the football results came on, then, as if guilty about his own inactivity, he would be back out to attend to his chores, all urgency and purpose.

The programme might start with a real wrestler like Mike Marino, an artist with strength, grace and all the moves, who would win cleanly and conventionally. Dad almost purred watching the artistry of this professional whose background was the sport of wrestling. Years of watching wrestling meant he knew a 'proper wrestler' when he saw one.

He accepted that all those entering the ring could actually wrestle and that most of them had skills, otherwise they could have been seriously hurt. But he disliked the showmen of the ring for what he called their 'poncing about': all the strutting and posing and the glittery robes, sparkly boots and shiny trunks. They would do victory laps of the ring, strutting and pouting with their chests puffed up, flexing their muscles. All before the fight had even started. He accepted it was the game, it was what the little old ladies in the ringside seats had come to see.

The comedy-drama would begin. The combatants for each bout would enter the arena to howls of derision, cheers and catcalls. They would whip up the spectators. The old ladies would scream at the fighters and sometimes swing a well-aimed handbag in a wrestler's direction.

Jackie 'Mr TV' Pallo would strut into the ring in a gold-lined robe and shiny white trunks, snowy white boots. Cocky and confident, he made a living as a pantomime villain between his wrestling commitments. He would spend ninety per cent of the 'contest' strutting round, egging on the ringside punters and goading them into a frenzy. Dad, now fully invested in the drama, would yell 'get on with it' at the telly. When Pallo did engage, he usually won. That he could actually wrestle was not in doubt, and Dad would wonder aloud why he couldn't just wrestle instead of all the 'pratting about'.

The arch baddy was Mick McManus, a short, round-chested barrel of a man. He snarled and growled at the crowd, threatening to come over the ropes and sort out whoever was giving him lip. By now, the old ladies, incensed by a particularly brutal piece of McManus thuggery, would be on their feet with their arms stretched under the bottom rope, screaming at the ref. McManus could actually wrestle, but preferred to menace his opponents before beating them to a pulp with forearm smash after smash. Dad was unimpressed.

As the TV audiences grew, so the wrestlers involved became more extreme caricatures. Many became household names, so popular was the wrestling at the time. Dad liked to think of himself as more of a purist, but he still watched the likes of Giant Haystacks and Big Daddy ply their trade.

The villains became even more villainous, the pretty boys even more camp and 'poncey' and slowly people stopped taking the 'sport' seriously. You knew just what to expect and the bad guys duly served it up every week. Eventually, the wrestling was no longer enough to keep Dad from his animals on Saturday afternoon.

Dad loved proper wrestling and John and I would form a tag team to take him on. Stripped to our pants before bath time, we would act out fights in the hallway as soon as Dad got in from the yard. He'd strip down to his underwear, hang his work clothes on the peg by the back door, and we would grapple for supremacy in the wide hallway at the bottom of the stairs. The hall had a glass-panelled front door, and one evening the local vicar came knocking. He was greeted by the site of two small, skinny boys in pants, grappling with a large hairy man, also in pants, yelping, screaming, feigning injury and trying out the latest moves from the telly. Mum, hearing the knock on the door, calmly stepped over the pile of sweaty bodies and answered, her embarrassment complete. We skittered upstairs – Dad included – to hide until the vicar was gone.

30

GREETHAM LODGE

By the late seventies the farm shop was starting to dominate the lives of the whole family. Dad resented the fact that he was no longer spending most of his time farming and was now the proprietor of a highly successful retail business. The ever longer days were wearing him out, and dealing with what he called, sarcastically, the Great British Public, or even worse 'the great unwashed' was starting to get on his nerves.

The decision was taken to sell Scout Dike and to look for a farm of the type that Dad had always dreamed of having: the 'dog and a stick farm' that had been his ambition from the very beginning. Dad was now in his early fifties and selling the property with a successful business now seemed to make this long-held dream a possibility.

By this time, I was away at university. I wanted to graduate and then make a start on what Dad called 'learning by other people's mistakes' by getting a proper job, before coming back to take on the farm shop and perhaps build my sausage empire, allowing him to get back to his farming. I am not sure that this would have ever worked. At the time, we were not really getting on and disagreed on pretty much everything. Our lives had diverged when I left for university. He never visited and we did not speak at all during term time unless he answered the phone when I made my weekly calls to Mum. I was grateful for the paid work during holidays to pay off my overdraft, but we had few conversations about my university life. He thought all students were long-haired drunkards and drug addicts and he didn't care to be proved wrong by coming to see for himself.

But in the back of my mind, the farm shop was a great business and my plans to build up a really profitable meat operation burned bright.

Dreams of becoming a banger millionaire were put on hold for a time while I started work as a graduate trainee with Northern Foods, a multi-million-pound turnover food company. Here I was to learn at others' expense. However, Mum told me over the phone during my weekly call home, that Dad had been down to an auction in Stamford and had bought a dairy farm near Oakham in Rutland. My ambitions to take over the shop died right there. In typical Dad fashion, he had not shared his plans.

Buying the new farm before selling Scout Dike was a huge financial risk and there were anxious times. We didn't even have any dairy cows on the farm at Scout Dike and a big investment would be needed in the new place to stock it and then make it pay. Rutland was as rolling and gentle as

Yorkshire was hilly and hard. The farm at Greetham bordered the A1 to the east. The other side of the A1, after a few small hills, were the pan-flat fens of south Lincolnshire, cut through by steeply banked rivers and dikes, and home to a totally different type of farming from that done in Yorkshire.

Greetham Lodge Farm had seen better days. The buildings needed upgrading and to make money the capacity of the farm had to be expanded considerably. The pasture was tired from lack of fertiliser and had to be made to grow more grass. The land was flat and reasonably well drained compared to the Yorkshire soils and most of it was immediately accessible from the farmyard.

Large, flat pasture fields, much bigger than the patchwork of small fields up north, were bordered by high hedges and mature trees. Deep stagnant pools, alive with frogs and newts, were surrounded by small clumps of trees clearly indicating where the water table lay. Being located on the eastern side of the country meant it was considerably warmer, less windy and also less wet; this dryer climate meant the ground baked hard in the summer. In hot summers there would be precious little grass for the cows to eat. In winter though, when an easterly wind would blow straight off the fens, it could be bitterly cold.

At the back of the farm was a site of special scientific interest, an ancient ridge and furrow meadow, the only known location in the county of a rare orchid and several rare grasses. This was a riot of spring flowers and in the summer, humming with insects and thick with birds. Grazing rights were severely restricted, and the meadows were the subject of regular visits from inspectors, keen to preserve this rare location. They came to make sure that the precious grasses were not being cleared wholesale by Dad's hungry cows until they had finished seeding.

There was a tiny damp farmhouse, not large enough for the family of five still living at home, so the Little Lads moved into a large stationary caravan. They were no longer little by this time, but Mum still referred to them as that. Both were well into their teens, and John had just turned twenty. The caravan was like an oven in summer and freezing cold the rest of the year. For Mum, it must have been like going back to Top of the Town. There was almost no kitchen and the porous stone walls made everywhere cold and damp; only a roaring fire in the grate in winter made it tolerable. In time, Dad would build yet another house on land adjacent to the farm buildings.

The priority was the serious business of making the farm profitable and that meant producing milk and that meant growing grass. The land was undernourished and the grass old-grown, stalky, and far from abundant. Ageing pasture was ploughed and reseeded with the latest high-performance grass lays. Re-seeding could be a risky business, because if the rain failed to fall and the seeds failed to germinate, the whole process would have to be repeated. But ample manure meant that it was not long before there was enough grass to feed the growing herd of dairy cows that Dad was acquiring from breeders, including some from our Grandad's farm.

It took much longer to sell Scout Dike then Mum and Dad imagined, and they found themselves running down the stock

206

and continuing to run the farm shop, as they needed the money to fund the bridging loan on the new place. More long hours added to the frustration as both now wished to be away from Yorkshire.

In the process of moving everything almost a hundred miles from the old farm to the new, it became apparent that Dad had never thrown anything away, ever, just in case it might come in handy, one day. All the usual excuses. After all, you never know when you might need a pile of rusty iron bars or a radiator grill from an old tractor, now long gone. And he didn't see having to move everything as a reason to throw anything away now.

Eventually, the farm and the shop at Scout Dike were sold, just in time, as money was running short. The risk Dad had taken in buying Greetham before selling up in Yorkshire was huge, and money was drained from the business, setting back the much-needed investment in the new farm. But at least the grinding routine of the shop was gone, dealing with customers who thought it was all right to phone up at all hours. The promise of being back with his animals, rebuilding the new place and restoring it to a profitable farming enterprise was all the incentive he needed to throw himself into working the long hours he had always worked. Getting on again.

Slowly but surely, Dad and John made progress and the farm buildings were repaired or rebuilt. Bigger, better and more modern buildings were added, and strips of concrete were laid as the farm expanded, adding ever more stock. Cows grazed peacefully in the front of the house on either side of the long lane, at the end of which a solid five-bar gate kept the outside world at bay.

John and Dad worked together all day long, but probably passed no more than a couple of dozen words, each content to be getting on with their jobs, all the tasks divided up between them wordlessly. Sam was away at college and Andy attended an agricultural college close by, so Dad and John ran the farm with the help of local farm workers who came and went; as ever, most of them were unable to live up to Dad's standards.

After the chaos of the move, the farming seasons started to dictate activity once again; calves were born, replacement heifers reared to be added to the milking herd, bull calves fed on the ample grass silage that the farm started to yield and pretty soon the number of animals started to exceed the land available. So more land was rented around the county for grazing. Later, a large flock of ewes would be added to take advantage of the ample pasture available locally to rent.

Daily, Dad would tour the peaceful county of Rutland, England's smallest. Rented grazing land was dotted all around the local villages. Animals needed to be counted, to make sure there were no escapees, water troughs checked, and fences mended where required. Feed might be taken out to supplement the grass keep. He would walk quietly around his stock, as content as he had ever been.

31

GOING AWAY

We had been in the car for about an hour. It must have been somewhere in the region of Stevenage when Mum said: 'I hope I have got enough to read on the plane. I did bring yesterday's paper and a book, but the book is in the suitcase'.

I had collected Mum and Dad from home early that morning to deliver them to Gatwick for a holiday of a lifetime in New Zealand. The trip was the fulfilment of a long-held ambition. They had never really travelled far and now, in their mid-sixties, they'd decided it was time. I am certain Mum had not thought through just how long a twenty-six-hour flight can be, or considered what she might do during those long hours. I suggested it might be a good idea to perhaps buy some magazines and books at the airport – we were hours early, and she would have ample time to browse the bookshops at the airport – but it seemed to be the expense that was putting her off.

'I'm sure I'll be OK with the paper, gives me chance to read it properly,' she said.

I am equally certain that Dad hadn't thought it through either. I had never seen him read a book in his life. Reading did not come easily, and he was out of practice, his butterfly attention span ill-suited to concentrating on something as long and time consuming as a whole book. To Mum, reading felt like a luxury enjoyed by people who had the time for such things. Dad had no idea what to do with twenty-six hours of complete inactivity.

Circling London, they were astonished that there were fields on *both* sides of the motorway. They had heard of the M25, but never been on it. All they knew of it, from the radio, was that it was one long, continuous traffic jam. How could it be that farming was taking place in such proximity to London? In their minds, the 'south' was a built-up area: an agricultural wasteland.

Inevitably, somewhere near Watford, Dad asked, 'Are we nearly there yet?'

A few minutes later he asked if there was a chance of stopping for the loo. Life had come full circle. I felt like saying, 'Of course we are not nearly there, you are going to New Zealand for Christ's sake. Be patient, relax, enjoy the journey.' But I smiled and bit my lip and pulled into the next services.

The flight to New Zealand was to be the first long-haul journey that they had ever undertaken. Dad had been on an aeroplane before, just once, with a bunch of other pig farmers, keen to learn the secrets of the Danish pig industry. This trip had been advertised in the *Farmers Weekly* magazine, and had an almost non-stop itinerary, packed full of farm visits and sightseeing around New Zealand's North and South Islands. This kind of relentless programme undoubtedly appealed to Dad.

I was certain that they would have no idea what to do when we arrived at Gatwick, so I parked and walked with them into the terminal, pointing them to check- in, finding the right desk and making sure that they were in the right queue. They looked small and vulnerable. They seemed terribly unsure, fidgety and nervous, totally unprepared and probably wishing they had stayed at home. I had never seen them so far away from their natural habitat. What had happened to my parents' ability to take everything on without breaking stride? After check-in I waved them off at the departure gate after the briefest of hugs from Mum and an uncertain thanks from Dad.

My Dad would always tell anyone who would listen that he thought he had had a good day if he had not left his beloved farm. Mum would wince at this, quite clearly longing to be anywhere other than the blessed farm at times, if only for a short while. But with the Yorkshire farm and the shop sold, and John now old enough and responsible enough to be left in charge, Dad had run out of excuses.

In New Zealand they visited huge dairy farms where the cows were outside all year round, where the milking parlour was an open-sided shed and was often the only building on the farm other than the house. This low input, low output, extensive farming model must have seemed totally alien to Dad, whose methods were highly intensive, hustling every bit of productivity out of the animals and the land. But New Zealand was blessed with a climate where grass would grow all year, which was very different from the land that Dad had farmed in Yorkshire.

They visited hill stations where thousands of sheep grazed on lush high pastures. The scenery was breathtaking, and they were warmly welcomed by fellow farmers. They completely forgot to take any pictures though, or to even remember much about the trip. They only saw the farming.

Some three weeks later, I was on taxi duty again. I waited apprehensively in the arrivals hall at Gatwick for them to emerge. Had they had a good time? Was New Zealand everything they had hoped; had it lived up to their 'trip of a lifetime' expectations? They strolled through the swing doors, seemingly a foot taller than when they left, now confident, seasoned travellers, relaxed and smiling. I felt like saying, 'Who are you and what have you done with my parents?' Nevertheless, my wonderful parents were relieved to be home, ready for some familiarity, having travelled well, but so ready for a nice cup of tea.

They had little to say about their experiences in New Zealand, no matter how hard I pressed for at least some impressions. They had plenty to say about the three day stop off in Fiji on the return leg of the journey. This was another matter altogether. Dad had lots to say about that:

'There was nothing to do!' he complained. 'Apart from sit in the sun and eat and drink, and then drink some more.' He was mystified: why did some of his fellow travellers need to be at least slightly inebriated if not blind drunk on every possible occasion while on holiday? Dad was teetotal all his life and he was genuinely baffled. I got the impression that friendships cemented in New Zealand quickly came unstuck in Fiji when Dad realised that his fellow travellers could 'drink like fish' as he put it through pursed lips, his puritanical, virtuous abstention (in his mind) setting him apart – above – those who needed a drink to have a good time.

But the main problem with Fiji was that there was simply no farming to look at: no fields, no work being done, no urgency, just a few cows tied to trees and a slow pace of life that a hot climate dictates. He could no more understand what Fiji was for than he could fly to the moon. The idea that people would travel thousands of miles to this warm, beautiful and friendly place, just to sit in the sun and drink beer, was alien to Dad. The whole concept of resting up on the journey home having had two and a half weeks of almost constant motion simply did not occur to him, all he wanted to do was to get back to work on his farm.

Sure enough, having travelled halfway round the world, somewhere near Watford, Dad asked me if we were nearly there yet, shortly followed by a polite request to stop for a pee.

New Zealand was the first of two 'farming' trips they went on: the following year they visited California. Again, organised for the benefit of a group of retired farmers, the California

trip was an opportunity to look at the American way of doing things. Dad came back from this holiday with a bad cough, which persisted for months before a scan revealed a fungal spore growing in his chest. This had to be removed along with part of his lung and, as a bronchitis sufferer all his life, he never really regained his old energy. The offending growth was promptly transported to the London School of Hygiene and Tropical Medicine who urgently wanted to analyse it and very soon after pronounced it very rare, a fact confirmed in a nice letter, thanking Dad for his contribution to medical science.

This episode marked the end of their international travel, as if the illness had confirmed in Dad's mind what he had known all along, that danger lay beyond his farm gate. I am sure that a fungal spore was not one of the many dangers he had imagined might come from going abroad, but it was enough. No more overseas adventures.

From then on, holidays for Mum and Dad consisted of snatched breaks, no longer then three or four days, where they would head up into the Yorkshire Dales or perhaps the North Yorkshire Moors. It must have been like seeing the same old movies over again, familiar, comforting and where you know the ending. Somewhere farming was being done in a way that he recognised, somewhere he could see over the hedges or the drystone walls into the fields and the farmyards: this was Dad's type of holiday, and Mum was just thankful to be away and have Dad's attention for a while.

But Dad was, as ever, restless, keen to take in as much of the

surrounding farming as possible, so they would never stop the car long enough to get out and walk a little. Maybe they would park on top of a hill, wind down the car windows and enjoy the view, perhaps with a sandwich or two. Contentment consisted of familiar country stretching out in front of them through the windscreen of the car, recognisable landmarks on the far horizon. Never again would they stray so far from home.

32

LIFE AND DEATH

Whichever way you look at farming it is a matter of life and death. On a livestock farm, new life is arriving all the time and death is ever present, whether by design or bad luck. Dad knew that if he looked after his animals properly then they would look after him and his family in return.

New life meant paying minute attention to his animals, through patient observation, being able to read the animals' behaviour, knowing when a sow would be ready to go to the boar, or a heifer old enough to visit the bull for the first time. Missing a cycle meant that there would be a delay in the next litter of pigs, or to the arrival of the next calf, which over the years would all add up and make substantial differences to the productivity and profitability of the farm. Dad would run his stockman's eye over his animals and know when it was time.

The sow would be ushered to the boar pen, grunting quickly but not loudly, excited, knowing exactly what was about to

happen. At this point I would make myself scarce, feeling the same prickly embarrassment you might feel sitting with your parents watching two people having sex on the telly. After all, I was not really supposed to know about what Mum called the birds and the bees. Mum and Dad never mentioned this to me or any of my brothers. Some of my friends had had 'the talk' and I am not sure whether to feel grateful that we never did, or resentful that my parents never felt it necessary. Of course, we all learned pretty much everything we thought we needed to know long before we left junior school, saving my parents and us the awkward embarrassment.

Sometimes animals would take more than one visit to the boar to conceive. These sows would be put on the 'watch list': what my dad called giving them 'The Scarborough Warning', another phrase I only ever heard him use, meaning a warning given much too late to be useful. Repeated failures would mean a one-way ticket to the abattoir and more raw materials for the sausages. Dad used all his senses to make sure that new life was growing inside his animals, and he would not hesitate to make decisions if not.

New life meant that he could continue to grow the farming business, more pork pigs to be sold to eager consumers, replacement heifers for the milking herd, or a bull calf that he could fatten for slaughter. It didn't always work though, and sometimes, come the morning, there would be a stone-cold dead calf stretched out on the ground outside the calving pens, eyes wide open and tongue lolling from its mouth, specs of its mothers blood darkening red against the animal's black-and-white hide. A dead calf was a source of frustration, grief, a sense of lost opportunity. A strong heifer calf would bring a smile. But life and death on a farm was an accepted cycle and you moved on. There was always more work to be done.

At Scout Dike, if a litter of pigs was taking an age to farrow, he would offer a helping hand. Maybe just one was facing the wrong way and had got stuck, holding up the birth of its brothers and sisters. As piglets spilled to the floor, he would gently use his fingers to clear the mucus from their noses, making sure their airways were open. Groggy ones were held in the palm of his big hand and given a quick rub, to get the blood circulating before placing them by a free teat for a first drink, or under the heat lamp to warm up, dry out and find their legs.

Sometimes he would gently scratch the sows' foreheads or behind their ears as they gave birth or rub their bulging tummies to soothe the process and stimulate the flow of milk. Success was a pink pile of sleeping new-born piglets under the heat lamp, lying content and full of their mother's first milk. I believe this was the excitement and the magic for him, but it was based on hard economics as well.

Keeping pigs could also be heartbreaking at times. Dad designed the farrowing pens with horizontal metal rails set into the walls either side of the sow. If the piglets needed to move out of the way when the mothers moved, they were able to escape behind these rails. People always say how intelligent pigs are, but at times it was impossible to believe this, as clumsy sows would often roll over and crush or suffocate their new-born offspring. At moments like these, all Dad's tenderness disappeared, and frustration boiled over into anger. I once saw him punch a sow so hard his hand must have almost broken. The thick-skinned animals were oblivious. Dad would have no hesitation in dispatching the almost-dead piglets, their ribs broken and crushed, struggling to catch their last breath. Holding their back legs in his hand, with a rapid swing, head-first into the nearest wall with a sickening thwack, they were put out of their pain.

Dad would sometimes go to great lengths to keep his animals alive. He had a cupboard full of syringes with huge needles and medicines for everything on the farm. He had taught himself the most elementary veterinary medicine. Real vets were hard to afford, but when one was called, Dad watched and listened and learned so he could do it himself the next time.

A premature death caused him real pain. After I left home, if I were to call and he happened to answer the phone, an enquiry as to his health would bring a report of a calf born dead that morning. And that is the inherent contradiction in farming. Stockmen show love for their animals but cannot afford emotional attachments. On sunny evenings he might be walking quietly among his beef cattle as they jostled gently for his attention, scratching them behind the ears and gently running his hands along their backs; the next morning he might be loading four or five of them into a trailer destined for the slaughterhouse.

Pigs that he had given life to, that he had reared from tiny, defenceless babies, that he had fed and watered and bedded down, making sure they were warm and comfortable, would be just as easily dispatched to the abattoir.

Here his animals became carcases, the cattle, headless and stripped of their hides, impossible to recognise as the ones we had walked among only hours earlier. Pigs, neatly halved along the length of their spines, were hung up by the back legs in long orderly rows in the slaughterhouse chill room, awaiting collection. They would be efficiently unhooked, slung over white-coated shoulders and thrown into the back of the van, taken back to the farm shop ready to be jointed and sold.

Our animals never had names – names were for people, horses and pets. Dad never lost sight of the fact that his animals were a means to an end, a way to earn money, make a living, grow the business and secure the future. For all that though, he still enjoyed their company and being among his animals somehow calmed him, gave him moments of quiet and relief from the ever-present need to press on with the jobs to be done.

33

GETTING OLD

Dad fell over on some ice in early 2002. It was not the first time he had fallen but this time was different. He was now seventy-two and had not been in great health since his lung surgery. His relentless work ethic had taken a heavy toll on his body. His back had been bad for as long as I could remember.

He had a series of slipped disks and trapped nerves, and even wore a surgical collar for a while. He supported his back with a tight metal-plated canvas corset, strapped tight around his middle. In pain almost constantly, he ploughed on with hard, physical farm work, and when he was able, even continued to sprint out of Speedway on a Thursday night to avoid the queue for chips. He sought out the latest treatments like deep heat and acupuncture – anything to gain a few hours' relief. He knew that doing less heavy work might relieve his pain, but he had no choice but to carry on.

Because of being on his feet most of his life, his knees had worn out, made even more painful by his rheumatoid arthritis. He had both replaced, causing him even more pain. A new knee meant huge, swollen joints and raised red scars for months. He never regained his mobility and was never steady on his feet again. The doctors told him that he was wearing out the new set of knee joints and would need a further round of replacements if he didn't let up. He took no notice and carried on as he had always done, cursing the pain and cursing how slow it made him, but not allowing it to stop him.

Burning pain in his legs kept him awake at night, and he was only capable of relief if he slept with his legs out of the bed. His whole body hurt at times. Anti-inflammatory drugs of increasing strength were prescribed, but he complained that these bunged him up and he would rather have the pain. Rheumatism wracked his shoulders. Disc damage meant his back was permanently out of kilter. And now the fall.

In my mind he was always so strong, so robust. Bomb proof. But even though it had been coming for years, it still came as a shock to see his capabilities reduced so suddenly. Like Samson with no hair, all the strength he had relied on was taken away. Just one misstep while down the yard, feeding his calves.

I wonder if he realised as he walked his fields on some inconsequential mission, probably now forgotten, that it would be for the very last time? Or when he had driven round the county to check on his cattle grazing on rented land, that he would not be able to do this again? Did he remember the last calf he had helped to drink from a bucket for the first time, patiently coaxing warm fresh milk into the new-born animal's mouth until it got the hang of it? He was now robbed of his strength. His will power could no longer overcome his physical shortcomings. He was not in the least bit prepared for this.

He was hospitalised for a while after the fall. He had gone down heavily, bruising his left side. His arm, hip and thigh were a riot of purple, yellow and blue as the bruises emerged. Worse still, the nerves that controlled his lower leg were damaged beyond repair and his foot had 'dropped', hanging at forty-five degrees to his ankle; there was nothing he, or any amount of physiotherapy, could do to remedy it. The doctors told him the nerves would take a very long time to grow back. Even in a healthy body, this was unlikely, such was the damage.

The fall changed him. We had met for lunch a few days before. I wanted to introduce him to my new girlfriend. He was impressed, saying none too subtly that he thought she was a 'looker'. At lunch, he had a twinkle in his eye, and I saw a glimpse of his old mischief. He had always known which button to press to cause me maximum embarrassment and that lunchtime he pressed every last one. I was transformed into an awkward, gawky kid again. He was charming as he flattered and amused in ways I had not seen for a long time. Annoying sod.

We never saw this side of him ever again. Perhaps it was the pain: not only the physical pain of his injuries, but the mental torment of the new restrictions on his movement. For one so active, this was probably the worst part of the situation he found himself in. The physical pain he could handle. He had

had it for so long. But now he couldn't stand without help and his foot dangled, so he needed a frame with wheels on it, which he hated and hid behind his chair out of embarrassment. His frustration boiled over. Enquiring how he was brought bitter rants about how useless he felt, how he was now a 'cripple, a waste of space'. This was not easy for any of us to hear and we eventually stopped asking.

As the months passed, the pain from the fall subsided enough to allow him to move around a little. Through regular physio his leg strengthened until he was able to slip on a special boot and make his way, agonisingly slowly, towards the yard and his beloved animals. In winter he would wear two big coats as he couldn't move fast enough to keep himself warm. But slowly he would haul himself round the calf pens, feeding the bigger ones, giving milk to the new-born and bedding them all down for the night. It would take him hours to do what used to take him minutes, but he was making himself useful. As hard as it was to be up and doing, it was a hundred times better than doing nothing.

I believe it caused him physical pain to be separated from his stock. The animals were his therapy. Just as other people do yoga or jogging, working his stock gave him an endorphin hit. But over the months of recovery, he had become unfamiliar to them and in turn, the farming clock had ticked on; for the first time there were animals on the farm that he had not had a hand in birthing, that he had not raised from calves himself.

By now John and the team on the farm were running things. Over the years, learning by example, he had become an accomplished stockman – although Dad would never admit it. That sixth sense was hard to pass on to the next generation. But John accepted the long days and the absence of days off. He milked the cows morning and night. Various farm workers came and went, picking up the jobs Dad would have done. John was the one who now drove around the county checking on the stock away on rented land. He was now the one taking only snatched holidays.

Dad felt entirely surplus to requirements, and over the years that followed, a combination of his lack of physical mobility and sheer lack of motivation resulted in him becoming almost entirely housebound, and therefore cut off from his farming life. Offers to put him in my car and drive him round to see his animals were met with a terse 'no thanks'.

The pressure on Mum was enormous as Dad became less and less able to help himself. He would struggle to get his arms at the right angle to get his own coat on or to lift them high enough to pull on his own hat. Meals would be prepared, but his appetite had vanished. He could do less and less for himself, but expected to be helped into his multiple layers of clothing so he could go down the yard for a couple of hours.

Mum had a very active social life, which she persisted with, even though she knew Dad would become extremely fretful almost as soon as she left, longing for her safe return. To her credit, she tried her best to continue with the village Women's Institute, where she was an honorary chairwoman. Dad slept a lot through the daytime hours, something he had never done before, then complained bitterly that he could not sleep at night.

He was not interested in watching television or reading. He never had been before, so why would he start now? In addition, he was going deaf, so any television was watched with the volume at an ear-splitting level for anyone else in the room. He was only concerned with what he could see by craning his neck to the right, to look out of the window at the comings and goings on the farm – and after a while, not even that.

He disliked being at all dependent. Refusing any offers of a steadying hand, he would try to stand and then to walk. This would lead him to fall often, and Mum would be unable to pick him up by herself. John would have to be called to get him back on his feet. Dad would offer searing self-recriminations about what a 'useless bastard' he was now and how he wished he was dead. Such was the anger in his voice and the conviction of his words, it became impossible to offer any words of consolation without sounding hollow and utterly unconvincing.

By this time I had moved further away and had been living for a while in Henley-on-Thames. Visiting home became a chore and happened less and less frequently. Thankfully John lived on the farm, and Sam and Andy were not too far away. But the Little Lads didn't visit that often either, like me perhaps unable to face the reality of Dad's decline full on, or just realising visits were a thankless task. I know Mum appreciated us going, and always went to great trouble to make a good lunch. But it was clear that Dad was changing, visibly shrinking before our eyes, but so slowly that those who saw him every day probably didn't notice as much. His strong arms withered and his neck became thin.

He boiled with resentment, flipping between anger and self-pitying helplessness: the opposite of the strong man he had been all his life. He took no joy from spending time with his family, and no pleasure from his many grandchildren. His bitterness meant we avoided spending time with him and did so only out of duty. Conversations, always a struggle, were now impossible as he had less and less to say. We never had the longed-for – by me – conversation between a father and a son where each offloads all the things they have wanted to say for years, if only there had been time.

His horizons narrowed rapidly to the corridor from his chair to the toilet to the bedroom and back again. He was incapable of getting far and it seemed that there was nothing of interest to him outside this narrow path any more. His eyes became blank and uncomprehending. In time, he gave up on going to bed, choosing to spend wakeful nights in his recliner. Any curiosity he had about the workings of the farm had evaporated.

Eventually it became impossible for Mum to look after him properly. After sixty years of being by his side, she could no longer do it. She had married him for better and worse, in sickness and health.

Accepting that she could no longer take care of him – in her mind – broke the unbreakable vows she had made, the lifelong and most solemn of obligations. In sickness and in health could have been added to with 'come hell or high water', or 'plague and pestilence', or any other combination of circumstances that life might have served up. To her, she had made the commitment to her husband. Now, she could no longer look after him and it diminished her, in her eyes, taking away her purpose and part of her self-worth with it.

Even with a steady stream of carers coming to the house to help, Mum was not really coping. I know it broke her heart to see the man that she had loved reduced to shouting for her every time she left the room. Even though she would be only feet away, Dad's growing confusion and anxiety prevented Mum from having any kind of life outside of his narrow corridor either.

Residential care was arranged, and Mum made her weary way to the care home every day. My brothers and I had awkward visits, stilted conversations which quickly tailed off. Perhaps it was the effect of the numerous micro-strokes he had been having or the painkillers that caused him to make no sense at all for long periods. I think we all wanted to deny the onset of Alzheimer's, although as the months ticked by, the symptoms of the disease became increasingly evident.

For one who made a virtue of forward motion, and work for the joy of making progress, to see him half propped up in bed, his body frozen by arthritis and rheumatism, was hard to take. He had always told us that the pain in his muscles and joints was less if he kept moving. Now he barely moved at all. His face became thin and his bones jutted from his joints. He was a shadow, and all the powers he possessed, physical and mental, were gone. With his jaw clenched tight and his chin jutting forward, his anger was palpable and his frustration filled the room, but there was nothing he could do about it, nothing he could even form into words any more.

The care home saw to it that he was as comfortable as he could be, but there was no physiotherapy to help him keep moving, and eventually he stopped eating much at all. He had always thought of himself as totally self-reliant, so the indignity of having to be fed was too much. Withering into his now tiny curled-up shell of a body, with parchment-thin skin, he appeared more like a fragile baby bird than the man he once was. His disinterest in everything was complete; a flickering TV, turned up uncomfortably loud, sat in the corner, completely ignored.

The window in his room was too high for even someone standing up to see out of, and the sun barely ever shone in on the sterile blank-white interior. Had he been able to see out of the window, he might have taken a little comfort from the animals that quietly grazed the fields surrounding the care home, but I doubt it.

I saw him for the final time three days before he died. Perhaps one of the senses I inherited from him told me that his death was probably only a matter of days. He had been diagnosing his animals in this way for years, forecasting their demise with uncanny accuracy. I told him that I loved him, something he had never been able to say to any of his sons. I told him that I knew that he was proud of us all, even though he never said so. All this was horribly late of course. His half-open eyes didn't flicker.

Dad's death was accepted by everyone as a 'blessed release', 'no more suffering', and all the other things people say to you when you lose a parent. I am not even sure that my brothers and I even missed him very much; we accepted the inevitable and were glad that he was no longer in pain. Our limited relationship with him during his final years meant there was no real gap that needed to be filled now he was gone.

In truth, he had left us at least a couple of years before, but this did not stop me blaming myself for feeling so little about his passing. Was I really as unfeeling as I imagined him to be towards us? I took myself to task for not saying things to him that I now wanted to say, too late. Should I have tried harder, been more patient? Probably.

For Mum, her beloved Bri was gone. Dad's passing left a hole in her life that no amount of getting on could fill. For more than sixty years they were together, indivisible, in harmony and lockstep. Their combined energy made two plus two equal five as they shored each other up. But she never cried. Not in front of anyone anyway. The iron self-control never wavered.

Together, they shared an unshakable belief in the joys of hard work and of progress made and of delayed gratification, paradise postponed. They would get to the top of the metaphorical mountain that they were climbing together. Did they ever sit, even for a short while and admire the view? I don't think so. Neither of them were good at quiet contemplation.

After Dad died, the usual arrangements were made and duly

passed by in a blur, none of us really pausing too long to consider whether Dad's life had been well lived. If a good life is spending most of your time doing something you love, then yes, he had a good life. If a good life is one filled with progress and growth, creating something, then yes. If a good life is spent with the woman you love and who loves you back, then, yes again. I don't think he would have changed it for the world.

I wrote and delivered a eulogy at the church, the heart of which provided the genesis for these stories. Dad would have thought that writing this was a monumental waste of time; he would have been embarrassed and dismissive about the good things contained here and would have nodded in ready acceptance of the bad things. He would have cautioned me against telling everyone 'his business'.

After the funeral and in the months that followed, very few words were spoken between Mum and her four sons and she tried to keep herself busy. For weeks after he died, it seemed she was still running at his pace. She chivvied herself along, as Dad was no longer there to do it, and she cursed her own lack of energy, her perceived inability to get things done, just like he would. She thought the concept of rest to be a sign of idleness. So three meals were prepared at the same times of day, every day, and she sat at the table as she had always done, as if unable to break from the routine, the way they had always done things together.

She busied herself with the things she had always done around the farm, making tea and cake for the workers, filling in the livestock movement records and even washing through in the dairy when there was no one else to do it. She would still go to Farm Women's Club and the WI, and to her once-a-month charity 'cancer lunch'. But she complained that all these things happened during the first week of every month, so she would be exhausted for a week, and lonely for the rest of the month. Activity on the farm went on around her, as ever, the relentless rhythms of the farming life.

I would ask her why she didn't invite her WI friends to tea, but she was firmly of the conviction that they all had better things to do than sit and natter with her. Like Dad, she didn't really hold with sitting or nattering when there was work to be done. I even pointed out that perhaps they were just as lonely as she was and might welcome an invitation. But she maintained she had jobs to do and that there never seemed to be the time.

When I visited, she would always tell me how behind she was with her jobs. She always made me a nice lunch and then slept most of the afternoon from the effort of it all, waking with a start to apologise profusely for her rudeness, sleeping when I had come all that way just to see her. We held hands as she slept. In truth, it was lovely to see her at last relaxed and at peace as she slept in the chair.

Instead of my regular once-a-week call, we now spoke two and sometimes three times a week. She was eager for news, any news, no matter how trivial, and I realised she was hanging on to her family, her way of belonging and prolonging.

Her identity as wife and partner for life had gone when Dad

died, but her identity as mother and grandmother lived on. I eked out the conversation with scraps of news from my family. When these ran out, we bemoaned the state of the country together: the lousy job the government was making of Brexit and that clown Boris Johnson. She read the *Daily Telegraph* cover to cover most days. She would complain that she was behind if she didn't get it read. But on visits, I increasingly noticed the papers piling up, unread, along with her magazines. Nevertheless, she remained both well informed and interested when we talked politics. Too soon though, our conversations would grind to a halt; she would become exhausted and leave me scrabbling for the next topic. In this way, she pretty much avoided talking about Dad at all, although I would bring things up that I had been writing about and she would claim she couldn't remember.

Mum continued to look after herself. I would gently remind her that she was in her late eighties and frankly deserved a rest. She had earned it. It became abundantly clear that she was no longer really fit to drive, and when her car needed a lot of work, the family decided that it should be sold – to her great resentment. Having spent most of her life never really complaining about anything much, she now felt the bitter loss of her mobility and realised that she had become reliant on other people's goodwill just to get around. She hated to 'put people to so much trouble'.

Mum's lifelong get-up-and-go slowly deserted her after Dad died. With no husband to look after, and with nothing to do other than, to her mind, the very slight task of looking after herself, her motivation evaporated. When Covid came along she became even more isolated. We dared not visit for fear of bringing the virus with us and the telephone became her lifeline. Not that she would ever phone any of us. We would be the ones doing the calling. She said she knew how busy we were and didn't like to interrupt, or that she never knew when a good time to call would be, so she almost never did.

Not wishing to be any trouble. Not wanting to create a fuss. Being concerned to interrupt when she knew we were busy. This was how she was. She never pushed her own opinions forward and rarely disagreed with anyone. Instead, she chose duty, to my father and to her family. Duty to support, to go along with Dad's plans, to endure the ups and downs and to be a constant, solid, reliable, hub, around which we all span.

She would fall quite often, usually because she refused to use her walking frame, or turned too quickly on her artificial knees and toppled over. She would hit the deck, sometimes catching a cheek bone on the corner of the work surface for good measure. Rheumatism in her shoulders and sciatica in her back caused her great pain. The doctors prescribed painkillers, the side effects of which were often worse than the pain she was in.

Much of the responsibility for looking after Mum fell to John and his wife Lesley, simply because they lived nearest, but this could never be a long-term solution and eventually she was not able to dress herself. Much to her embarrassment, frustration and great annoyance, carers were employed to come in four times a day to make sure she had everything she needed. Always intensely private, she disliked the seemingly constant stream of people who arrived to take care of her. Never the same person twice and clearly always on a tight time scale, the carers did what they had to do and left quickly, making the whole process even more impersonal and intrusive that it already was. She hated the very concept of people having to care for her.

After several trips back and forth to hospital, the family reluctantly decided that there would be no option but to have mum looked after by a local care home. This coincided with the rapid spread of Covid. She could not be discharged home from hospital as she could not care for herself. Over the previous months, her health issues had multiplied, compounded by the rapid onset of a great deal of confusion, which upset Mum and the family. Her lucid periods became fewer.

Covid drove the care homes to shut up shop, and visitors were not allowed at all, deepening the sense of solitary confinement that Mum must have felt. She complained of being abandoned. Snatched telephone conversations were all there was, and she often didn't make sense. We were allowed to stand outside her window and try to hold a conversation at one stage. This must have confused her further, and we recognised in her the same pattern of decline that we had seen in Dad's final months.

She struggled to come to terms with her new surroundings and with the fact she could no longer feed herself. Her sense of isolation became complete when she could no longer walk, the care home seemingly too short of staff to get her out of bed and into a wheelchair to enable her to socialise with her fellow residents. As the weeks passed, she grew thinner and more fragile, I am sure her carers feared to move her, worried she might break.

Mum died in early January 2022. She never recovered from the death of my father; how could she? Why would she? I found that I missed her far more than I expected. I would find myself still making mental lists of things to tell Mum about, only to remind myself, with a hollow, empty feeling, that she was not around any longer to tell these things to. Our triumphs and disasters, the successes of her grandchildren, things that I knew she would have taken delight in, could no longer be shared. For so many years, she had just been there, the constant – if at times slightly aloof and distant – presence in our lives, uncomplaining and undemonstrative, providing a guiding light by example, never with words.

34

AFTER WORDS

Stuff Dad Liked:

His animals
Mum
His sons (sometimes)
Working
Early mornings
Progress
Being able to see the results of a day's labour
Not having to leave the farm
Practical jokes
Motorbikes
Little Richard
Ray Charles
Glenn Miller
Driving fast

Stuff Dad Didn't Like:

Time wasters
Laziness
Sitting down
Chatting
Anything that held him up.
A problem he could not solve
Asking for directions
His mother-in-law
Going out – or at least the idea of doing so
Leaving his farm, even for a day
Holidays – he couldn't see the point
Smoking
Drunkenness

Stuff Dad never did:

Saunter, amble or stroll
Call any of his children by their proper names
Cut anyone any slack (unless he suspected they'd had a hard
time in earlier life)
Use words, where actions spoke louder
Slow down (voluntarily)
Drink alcohol
Small talk
Anything he didn't really want to do
Make a mobile phone call
Use a computer or surf the internet ('all just porn and filth')
Cry
Ask for help

About the Author

Mike Kirby is an entrepreneur, writer and long distance cyclist. He lives in Oxfordshire.